To Sherry,

With Love &
dreams that are
never gone up
Believe in you!

With Blessings
Joy

GETTING TO KNOW YOU

THE INTIMATE CONNECTION

Getting To Know You

The Intimate Connection

Kay Francis

BookPartners, Inc.
Wilsonville, Oregon

BookPartners, Inc.
P.O. Box 922
Wilsonville, Oregon 97070

Dedication

I dedicate this book to my two favorite people in my life … my children. No words can express the gratitude I feel for the faith you have shown in me. Your continuous support and humor made my job as a parent easier.

Through you I learned that our children are only on loan to us, never meant to be owned, therefore making me appreciate even more the loving and fun relationship we share together out of choice. Thank you for choosing me. I love you.

Acknowledgement

I regret that I am unable to acknowledge everyone connected to this book. For those whose names are not mentioned, please know that I am deeply grateful for your contributions.

I especially want to thank my good friend and associate, Sandra Roscoe, for believing in this project and encouraging me to write this book if for no other reason than for the pure experience of the adventure.

To Vickie D'Lamore, whose continuous nagging was responsible for my first draft. To Adair and Brad Hagar, my dear friends who introduced me to the world of computers and spell check. To Kate Warner and JoAnn Rossman, for their helpful hours of editing and humor.

To my mom for listening.

To the men who shared their perspective and comments, solicited and not solicited.

Special thanks to my dear friends Reggie and Joel, who introduced me to my publishers and fed me in their car as they chauffeured me.

A loving thank you to that special friend who opened my heart, and to my dear, dear friends of many years, Ceilie and Jack. To Fran Stubbs, who for the past twenty years insisted this day would become a reality.

To Thorn and Ursula Bacon, my publishers, who believed in my manuscript.

Thank you to Dr. Jay Spechler for reviewing my program and writing the foreword and to Marilyn Spechler for her valuable input and vote of confidence.

Last, but never least, a very special thank you to each of my clients. It was a privilege and an honor to be invited into your lives and to experience your inner strength and determination. Each of you taught me something more about the process of self-growth, and through you I learned the value of faith, forgiveness and unconditional love.

And in memory of my partner, Janet, and my friend, Jeff.

Table of Contents

Foreword

~ ~

In writing *Getting To Know You,* Kay Francis has developed a unique and effective model to aid an individual's understanding and effecting change connected with gender biases, prejudices and unproductive negative beliefs.

The book is filled with metaphors and anecdotes that help to make individual awareness and learning an easy and pleasant experience. It also emphasizes the necessity for each of us to challenge our potential and to grow emotionally and spiritually by achieving a balance between the latter needs. The thrust of the book's message is that by looking inward to identify and acknowledge our own biases, prejudices and negative beliefs, we can increase our awareness and sensitivity and move in positive directions.

There are also substantial benefits in applying Ms. Francis' model at the organizational or group level. As former director of quality assurance/engineering for American Express Company, my area of expertise is Total Quality Management (TQM). I have served as a Senior

~ ~

Examiner on the Malcolm Baldrige National Quality Award Committee, am currently a Judge for the State of Florida's Sterling Quality Award, and serve as a Judge for the U.S. Department of Energy's Quality Award. The model presented in the book addresses at least two very important aspects of quality management as described within all of the quality awards listed above. The first aspect that it addresses directly is that of human resource development and management. This part of the quality award's criteria is concerned with diversity in the workplace. The second aspect that it addresses is that of the need to promote teamwork. Applying the principles found in Ms. Francis' book would serve to create an enhanced awareness of an additional path toward achieving organizational teamwork, and it provides the tools needed to achieve it.

– Jay W. Spechler, Ph.D., P.E.

Introduction

~ ~

Getting to know someone intimately is not always easy. In fact, many people discover they feel anxious whenever they find themselves becoming more intimate within a relationship. On the other hand, there are those who feel awkward or uncomfortable when they meet or work with people who are different from themselves. Why is this? Why aren't all relationships easy and comfortable to manage?

Getting to know ourselves and other people should be a stimulating, worthwhile experience, one that leads us to become more understanding, caring, and emotionally mature.

Throughout our lives we share many different types of relationships and on many different levels, some more intimate than others, and some less important. But all relationships, regardless of their nature, depth, or intensity, deserve our attention. The people who touch our lives or whose lives we touch deserve our willingness to connect ...

a connection that fosters awareness, sensitivity and respect for ourselves and for them.

As a therapist, it is critical for me to possess the ability to build rapport and connect with clients on a more intimate level while, at the same time, remaining separate, nonjudgmental and objective. However, outside of certain professional settings the skill of remaining separate or set apart from another person can be an impediment. All people, professional or non-professional, should be cautious not to let this skill become a pattern of behavior. Remaining aloof or protecting yourself from being vulnerable may appear to be a reasonable strategy in certain situations, but in most relationships it's self-defeating and limiting.

As you read the following chapters, I think you will begin to understand the benefits to be gained when you open yourself to new ideas, thoughts and feelings as a natural way to experience yourself and others more intimately.

GEM, the *human needs model* presented in this book, is intended to help you rediscover yourself and reevaluate some of the ways in which you think about yourself and other people. GEM is the same model I use as a management consultant in the workplace. I use it as a training tool to help develop stronger teams, create better employee and customer relations and to maximize the unique talents of a diverse work force. As you begin to understand this human needs model and the philosophy involved with it, it will become more apparent why applying the model in your personal life and work life will help you to achieve higher levels of effectiveness and success.

You'll discover in the book information about yourself that you may be denying, overlooking, repressing or which you may feel is unimportant. So settle back with this book,

~ ~

and discover. Enjoy a new and different look into yourself, realizing there is hidden information about yourself worth uncovering. This information, once brought to conscious awareness, can help you build a stronger, more effective you.

Begin your contemplative, self-reflective tour with an open and curious approach. This is a great opportunity for you to learn more about yourself.

I have enjoyed sharing the anecdotes of my clients and the stories of the women and men I interviewed. It is because of these people that this book became a reality. For the protection of these people their names and identities have been changed.

~ ~

Chapter One

Getting To Know You

~ ~

Kimberly is a thirty-nine-year-old woman, divorced eight years and rearing two children, ages fourteen and seventeen. She earns her primary living as a computer programmer by day, and in the evening she offers computer support as a way to generate additional income. She entered counseling wanting to learn skills that would help her develop more meaningful relationships. Kim's appearance belied that of a woman struggling or suffering. She stood close to six feet in height, carried herself gracefully and with what appeared to be an air of confidence. She was soft spoken, and I could easily recognize her as a kind-spirited person.

Although she gave the outward image of being in control, her shallow breathing and tightly folded, wringing hands told me that she was experiencing discomfort and physical tension. Throughout our first session she frequently broke visual contact with me by lowering or shifting her eyes. But whenever I bent my head to write in

~ ~

my notes, I could feel her eyes staring at me. From the onset, I knew I was dealing with a cautious and fearful woman who was going to evaluate me every bit as much as I was evaluating her.

Kim stated she was lonely and depressed and felt that her life was nothing more than a "boring uneventful existence." She talked about her discomfort with the dating scene and described most of the men she dated as either insensitive or emotionally unavailable. Kim went on to say, "I'm even dissatisfied with my women friends. They never call me, it's always me reaching out to them."

In general, Kim felt the relationships in her life fell short of meeting her needs and expectations.

Kimberly was the oldest of five brothers and sisters. She spent the greater part of her teenage years caring for her siblings, providing them with as much nurturing as she was capable of giving and which was not provided by her parents. Essentially, Kim ran the household for her mother whom she referred to as "the closet alcoholic" and a father whom she said she didn't particularly know, stating, "he was just there."

As Kim began identifying and exploring her feelings she became saddened, angry and upset. During one of her sessions she blurted out in a childlike angry voice, "People aren't interested in me, they don't value my opinions, they don't even care about me."

It was during this session that we began looking at how Kim thought of herself. It was obvious that the picture she had painted was that of an unhappy and unattractive woman ... a picture she had furnished with the memories of her unhappy childhood.

Jeffrey is a forty-seven-year-old architect who was suffering from severe anxiety attacks. Initially, he was uncomfortable with the idea of seeking help, but as he put it, "I can no longer handle these attacks. I'm afraid I'm going to have a heart attack."

Jeff and his wife of seventeen years are the parents of three children ages two, ten, and twelve. Before the birth of their first child, it was agreed that his wife would give up her teaching career to become a full-time homemaker and mother.

A short time into therapy, Jeff divulged that he was involved in an affair with a much younger woman and wasn't sure if he wanted to stay in his marriage. His wife was feeling anxious about Jeff's lack of affection toward her, and his girlfriend was pressuring him to get a divorce. Jeff's cultural and religious background strongly disapproved of divorce under any circumstance, but especially for a reason such as another woman.

Jeff described his parents as polite to one another, but not loving. "I never saw any affection between them, and not unlike my wife and me, they never seemed to have any fun together. I don't want to end up like them. My wife's only interest is the kids, and other than that, we have little in common. She's a good person and a great mother, but she constantly reminds me how she took a back seat in order for my career to flourish. I suppose there's some truth in that, but she never exhibited any great desire to do much of anything. Truthfully, I hate weekends and I count the hours until Monday. I think I would go crazy if it wasn't for my work."

As we continued to explore Jeffrey's feelings, he began expressing reasons he felt entrapped. "I'm sick and tired of hearing about my obligations to my family. I've heard about family responsibility and obligation all of my life. My father complained about how hard he worked to

~ ~

provide for us, yet he seemed to judge himself and measure his success by how much he provided. I always remember him saying how he 'hung-in' *regardless.* I never understood what he meant by regardless. Regardless of what? My mom never let a day go by without reminding my brother and me of the sacrifices she was making to keep the family together, *regardless.* Now it's my wife telling me about my obligations as a family man. I'm sick of it. No question, I love my children, but does that mean I can't enjoy my life?"

I asked Jeffrey to take a deep breath to help calm the anxiety that was beginning to bubble up as he recalled certain events. It became obvious that Jeff was tapping into that deeper place where feelings, distortions and painful memories are buried and too often left unaddressed. As we continued talking, Jeff struggled more and more not to lose control. I could literally feel how hard he was working to contain all of the emotion that was working its way into his consciousness. It wasn't surprising that this caring but confused man was suffering from severe anxiety. Forty-seven years of repression and denial often leads to such extreme symptoms.

During my many years as a psychotherapist, clients like Kimberly and Jeffrey presented me with their confusion, emotional pain and internal conflicts. They weren't suffering from severe mental disorders, nor did they require psychotropic drug therapy. For the most part, they were women and men much like yourself, who functioned well in the outside world. However, for various reasons, they didn't feel their lives were working. These interesting women and men had specific needs. They realized there were aspects of their personalities or situations in their lives that needed improvement. They were eager to learn how to go about promoting this improvement rather than remaining unhappy or suffering from such feelings as fear, guilt, anxiety, depression or anger.

The GEM Model

Because of my clients, I decided to develop a model and approach that would address their special needs in ways that the more traditional psychotherapies either didn't emphasize or overlooked altogether, a model and approach that was gender-sensitive. So I developed the Gender Education Method, a *human needs model* designed to make this often hidden process more understandable and readily available. Through this model I wanted to reach two major goals: 1) to be sensitive to the unique issues and needs of both women and men; and, 2) to include in my assessment the different biases and prejudices that were a part of my clients' gender, culture, race, sexual orientation, ethnicity and religion. This more specific and personal information offered my clients and me additional insights into their issues and greater understanding of the particular ways in which they perceived themselves and others. It also helped my clients recognize how self-defeating and destructive it is to relationships to operate out of bias or prejudicial thinking.

GEM is a practical model and method for those seekers, those curious individuals that believe in personal development. It's a guide, if you will, to help access the internal resources that are critical in attempting to reach your "truth" and challenge your potential. But before you can make use of these internal resources, you must first be able to make the distinction between *wanting* to change versus *needing* approval. This distinction is important because change isn't an option until an individual is motivated and willing to grow beyond her or his need for approval.

It has been my professional experience that "self-growth" is seized by people who have guts, desire and discipline, people who try to look at themselves with an objective, examining eye and who possess enough ego strength to accept that they consciously or unconsciously operate out of a certain amount of bias and prejudice. They are people who acknowledge that they have some insecurities or personal weaknesses that need to be addressed, and they recognize the importance of confronting self-imposed limitations in order to develop healthier ways to get beyond them. They understand that the exciting (though, often disarming) process of honest self-disclosure is essential if they hope to achieve greater personal effectiveness, contentment and success.

GEM, my human needs model, offers new understanding and hope to anyone willing to rid him/herself of some antiquated and often confusing concepts. GEM helps you to hear a new inner voice, one that is open and curious about what is unfamiliar and different, a voice that is non-judgmental, free of the biases and prejudices we learn as children and which, as adults, we use to hobble our own personal growth.

Each chapter is filled with information, ideas and activities designed to help you create more authenticity and clarity in the areas of life that count: relationships, professional development and personal satisfaction.

Whether you read this book as a way to increase your effectiveness and success in personal relationships or in your career, remember: you can never improve anything in your life without first improving yourself. It's sort of like the Law of Gravity. It just *is*.

Chapter Two

GEM: A Model for Effective Living

~ ~

GEM is a visual aid designed to help you understand and work with balancing what I call the six basic requirements of human motivation. These are: Self-Love, Self-Power, Intimacy, Solitude, Equality and Manipulation. Although these six human needs aren't as vital for us to satisfy as is our need for food, water and shelter, they are vital in shaping our attitudes, beliefs and behavior.

GEM works because the six needs that it embraces are both universal and sensitive to difference. This model acknowledges similarities and, at the same time, respects and encourages individual uniqueness.

Applying the teachings of GEM helps free you from the stereotypical thinking that negatively affects your understanding and communication with others. GEM is the tool to help you discover what stops you from getting what you really need and want.

The Six Critical Relationship Needs

Self-Love: a liking for, and satisfaction with yourself; a sense of self-value, self-respect and self-appreciation.

Self-Power: a belief in your own abilities and the skills to develop yourself; it is the capacity to enlarge your range of choices, which creates personal change.

Intimacy: the capability for honest self-disclosure; it is the ability to trust yourself and others in order to experience close and deep levels of communication; an absence of fear that allows you the freedom to be vulnerable.

Solitude: the inner strength to stand alone when necessary, it is a sense of independence and internal self-control that implies competence to deal with life.

Equality: the conviction that you are unique, that your contribution in life is valuable to yourself and to others and that you and all people are of equal value as human beings.

Manipulation: the ability to exercise Self-Power to create positive change, to influence and control your personal environment; it is the intuitive quality of knowing your needs and those of others and working to meet those needs.

How GEM Works

Study the diagram of the GEM Model in Figure 1. Observe how the six needs are paired together to describe three separate relationships.

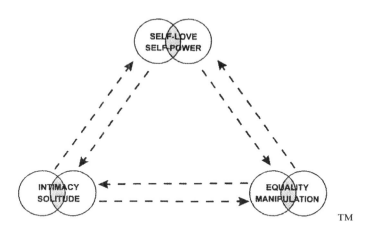

Figure 1.
Six Basic Needs of Interpersonal Relationships

The shaded area of the overlapping circles represents the ideal balance between Self-Love and Self-Power, between Intimacy and Solitude and between Equality and Manipulation, illustrating the importance of operating equally out of all needs. The arrows running both to and from each of the three sets of relationships indicate their interdependence.

The order in which we build these relationships is important. You can't develop a strong balance between Intimacy and Solitude until you are able to satisfy and balance Self-Love and Self-Power. You can't appreciate your Equality and Manipulation needs and how they work together before developing a strong sense of Self-Love, Self-Power, Intimacy and Solitude.

GEM stresses the importance of creating balance between these six internal needs, because being out of balance in any phase of your life can cause unnecessary turmoil that becomes a barrier to self-accomplishment and

~ ~

success in all phases of life. Internal balance gives you the strength to cope. At times, life may seem unfair and out of whack, but the right balance lets you move through life's inequities with determination and the belief that happiness and fulfillment are obtainable.

Understanding GEM will help create balance in your life. Sometimes, we may be okay in one area but not in another. We may think we're fulfilling one of the needs when we're really not. For example, women may experience what they perceive as Self-Love, yet remain unfamiliar with the experience of Self-Power. Their perceptions of Self-Love may or may not be accurate because they may not have a reliable gauge, and the "Self-Love" they feel may be lopsided without the equilibrium provided by Self-Power. For men, Intimacy is often thought of only in its sexual connotation. But to be most effective, Intimacy must also be experienced as an honest, skillful form of communication. At the same time, the fear of Solitude may be overwhelming. Standing alone may seem impossible. Both problems result from not knowing how to fulfill and create balance between the basic needs of Intimacy and Solitude.

Balance At Home

Home life should provide warmth and security. Whether you live in a single rented room or on an estate, whether you live alone, with a partner or with your family, your home needs to be a "soul shelter," a place where you can live in peace. It should be a sanctuary; safe, non-competitive and relaxing. Knowing how to kick back and drop out of life, if only for an hour, is extremely important. When your needs are in balance, you will automatically begin creating and inviting harmony into your home life.

Balance At Work

Internal balance stabilizes you when the pressures and demands at work become unbearable. One secret for enjoyment and success in the work world is to be comfortable enough with yourself that you can remain reasonably unaffected by the negativity of people and situations. Being centered and in balance at the job enables you to experience those aspects of your personality which are creative and innovative. If you manage other people, internal balance is calming, it motivates others and brings out the best in them.

It is unlikely that any of us has these six needs perfectly balanced at any given time, but the more you strive to create this internal balance, the more effective, productive and satisfied you will be in your job as well as in your personal life. Discovering where you are out of balance between these six needs is the first step. If you can acknowledge the existence of imbalance, bringing yourself into balance becomes easier.

Chapter Three

Developing Our Identities

~ ~

As with Kimberly and Jeff, what happens to you early in life plays a major role in determining your beliefs, attitudes, biases, and prejudices. Your self-identity begins to take shape as soon as you're born, so objectively exploring your early days will give you a better understanding of yourself.

Most women and men have only a vague sense of their self-identities, which were fostered in early childhood. As children, we are not intellectually equipped to question much of what we learn from the important adults in our lives. Instead, we take things literally and interpret information or actions as factual realities. As children, our emotions and feelings outweigh our intellect; we depend mainly on those feelings or on the reactions we observe in others as our guide for processing information.

At the stage in our childhood when we asked "Why?" about everything, the important adults in our lives handled questions in different ways. Some were patient and took the

~ ~

time to listen carefully to our questions. These same adults supported and encouraged our curiosity through their thoughtful and concerned answers. Other adults were either too busy or too insensitive to recognize the significance of our questions, so they did not respond with careful consideration of our developmental stage. Whatever information we did receive, and believed, may have been incomplete or even wrong.

Almost every question a child asks is significant because in our newly developing brains, everything has meaning. The adults in our world were our teachers, our mentors, so their answers and their behavior, which was often in conflict with their words, became vital information in our development. We were beginning to form pictures of ourselves and our relationship with the world. Our self-identities were evolving and taking shape.

We continue the process of self-identification throughout our lives, always accumulating new experiences and information. We depend on this information and from it we form opinions and pictures of who we are. The sources of information may change, but we still learn from listening and observing. We are affected by everything we think, feel and do.

Unless circumstances force us to challenge and question who we are, we hold on to beliefs and values that may be outdated, but more significantly, may be based on faulty information and perceptions. When we stop searching for new information, we become locked into a single, unchanging picture.

Who we are and what we're about may be different in reality from what we think. These distortions are often rooted in faulty messages we received about ourselves from parents, teachers, religious leaders, and others, and they

~ ~

sometimes stem from cultural values, prejudices and gender biases.

To get an accurate picture of what you think and feel, you need to understand and confront the messages you once blindly accepted. To do this, let's explore some of the forces and opinions that may have shaped your concept of yourself.

How Men Are Socialized

For most men, the drive to be successful and effective took root during early childhood. The pressures and demands of a fast-growing, complex society are both a result of and a dubious reward for that drive. The more men succeed, the more they are "rewarded" with even greater demands and expectations.

Although men experience a sense of power from their achievements and accomplishments, their effectiveness is restricted by a requirement to comply with what their social system says is "correct" behavior.

It's more difficult for men to be effective in their personal lives than in their work lives because society restricts their range of behavior at home more than it does at work. Men are socialized into adopting attitudes, beliefs and behavior that work against their ability to accept Intimacy in their personal lives.

Men are expected to provide for and protect the people who depend on them. At the same time, they are expected to set rules for wives and children to follow. Nothing in the deal, except for (maybe) the preacher's words at the wedding, says that it's okay for them to be loved and protected by the women in their lives. Yet human effectiveness depends on a balance between taking care of

~ ~

others and being taken care of. Because many men reject or don't even possess this balance, they become more ineffective.

Men are socialized to be the heads of households. This is a mixed message for both the men and their families because work pressures and obligations keep them outside the traditional household more than inside. They are looked to as the final decision makers when it comes to disciplining the children. But usually they're not on the scene when the incidents that require the discipline occur. Therefore, they are often seen by their children as villains to be respected out of fear.

Some men try to resist the old messages and become deeply involved in their home lives. While a man may satisfy his need for emotional fulfillment, it usually diminishes his success in competing against men who devote all their time to work. Too often, the men who become heavily involved in their home lives suffer the consequences of less financial success, less power and less acceptance from their peers. For some men, these consequences create a sense of failure, a conviction that they're not as effective in life as they should be.

Mixed Messages

Emotional sensitivity is often considered a weakness in our "machismo" culture. This isn't always the fault of males. Men often receive or perceive mixed messages about sensitivity from the women in their lives.

Women want men to be more sensitive, but men are not sure exactly what women mean by "sensitive." Some women want men to be more in touch with their feelings, to express their emotions more freely, to confide their inner thoughts to women. But, when men try to be more emotionally sensitive, they quickly learn that there is a line of acceptable behavior over which they can't step. If a man becomes too emotional or sensitive, the same woman who encouraged this behavior may start feeling uncomfortable. Depending on her bias, she may be worried that "her" man is going to fall apart.

With such conditioning, some men come to believe that sensitivity is good as long as they don't overdo it. It's okay to get misty-eyed over a highly emotional or romantic experience, and a few solitary tears may even be admired, but God help the man who lets the tears flow out of control, screams or reaches out to hug his wife for comfort. He's supposed to be *strong*. Women want men to be more sensitive, but not so sensitive that they'll lose respect for them as "men."

Which message should men listen to, the message of emotional expression and sensitivity or the one of self-control and repression? Because they've been taught since childhood to maintain control, they find it easier to heed the latter.

Sensitivity means more than men being able to express emotions and feelings. It means that women want men to be sensitive to women's needs. They want them to listen, to understand, to empathize. They don't want them to act always as leaders, to solve their problems. They want what *they* themselves give to men.

This certainly is not an unreasonable request, and women can't understand why men find it so difficult. Many men try hard to please, but they often fail because pleasing others and building relationships was not a part of their early training. Women are asking them to do something they never learned to do.

Competition

Some men must be in charge and in control at all times to feel effective. They need to perform because the better they perform, the more reinforcement they receive for being successful. This type of socialization implies that who you are is far less important than what you do.

Competing is a natural process for men, and their "system" is built around it. Society views competition as a healthy outlet for men and a legitimate source of excitement. On the surface this isn't such a bad thing. But when some men try to extend their lives, growing past the need to compete as aggressively as they were brought up to believe they should, they are often viewed as not masculine. American society has emphasized such things as getting a good education, performing well in business, making money, acquiring material goods and participating in politics as measures of success for men. Many men still accept the adage that "the one with the most toys wins." They push themselves to goals they can't possibly attain, at least not without severe consequences to health, family or psychological well-being. Even when they reach these "bigger than life" goals they're still left with a feeling that there's more to obtain or achieve. When they don't reach these unrealistic goals, they feel inadequate. Either way, they're left with a sense of incompleteness. They generally choose not to deal with this incomplete feeling, so they just go on doing more of the same.

The traditional male role involves aggressive behavior, rationality and logical thinking. Emotional feelings and expression are not acceptable or understood so men typically suppress these unwanted and uncomfortable feelings.

Role Models

Most boys look to their fathers as role models. But many boys never have the chance to interact with their fathers because the fathers are absent because they are too busy working. These boys never know their fathers intimately, because to get to know someone intimately, the other person must be willing to expose himself and become more vulnerable. Lucky is the young man whose father, in spite of the socialization process, validates and expresses his own emotions, and encourages his son to do the same. Men who were physically, sexually or mentally abused as children often repeat this behavior in their own relationships. This mimicry also reinforces the suppression of emotions in their children, extending the cycle to yet another generation.

Mid-Life Crisis

Men often experience a dilemma we call a "mid-life crisis." At this stage, some men believe their lives are flawed because they failed to accomplish the Great American Dream. Many react to this self-imposed crisis by behaving in a way that, while natural, is destructive, because it leads to an even greater sense of failure. They cope by adopting the behavior they learned as boys, when they were taught to become independent.

During the growing up process, boys are forced away from the warmth, love and protection of their mothers. They learn not to depend on their parents and to concentrate on the lessons of individual achievement. Ridding themselves of dependency is part of the growing up experience for boys. It's easy to understand why men would not seek nurturing relationships to help them cope with mid-life crises; after all, it would seem unnatural for a grown man to become too dependent on his partner or children.

So during this vulnerable time, some men break away from their greatest sources of comfort. They break away from relationships at work by quitting their jobs or by changing their careers. They often destroy their relationships at home by leaving their partners or other people who best understand them. During this difficult time in men's lives, they may even leave the relationships in their community by moving away, and, in so doing, they topple what little balance they had in their lives, rather than trying to solve their problems by bringing their needs into better balance.

A Changing World for Men

More than ever, men are questioning how they have allowed themselves to be socialized in their personal lives and at work in ways that ignore their emotions and deny their abilities to be intimate with themselves and with others.

When men are exposed to a different world from what they once knew, the perceptive ones learn that old beliefs don't work in a new system. They challenge themselves in new ways as they realize that their internal needs must be met.

Because they are open to new ideas, they can change, although it may not seem easy. They're not accustomed to looking inward, to sorting through the past, to challenging what they were led to believe was their birthright. But they can make the changes, and it isn't nearly as difficult as they may imagine.

~ ~

A Man Who Thought He Had Failed

Ken lost his job after fifteen years. He had turned the dying company around through his innovative and cost-effective programs, but that meant little when new management took over and asked, "What have you done for us lately?" At age fifty, Ken was deprived of the rewards of his accomplishments. He felt betrayed, shut out, angry. But he was out of touch with the real conflict brewing inside. Though his wife worked and brought in a substantial income, this brought no comfort to Ken, because he was socialized to be the family "breadwinner." He withdrew and began to drink heavily, and, as things went from bad to worse, he stopped trying to get a new job. He ignored the pleas of those close to him, separating himself from his real needs.

For Ken, growing up had been relatively easy. His mother had always adored him, and although he described his father as "passive," he had been comfortable with their relationship. College wasn't for him and he left it after one year. The business world was his greatest joy. He had thrown himself into his work, climbing to the top with determination and paying little attention to his emotional needs, only grabbing the pleasures of life as they presented themselves. His focus had been on his career and his need for financial success.

Ken had married, not out of any desire to fulfill his need for intimacy, but, as he put it, "to be part of the program." Although he had felt tied down by his marriage, he wanted to be a father and felt he had picked a good mother for his children. He managed to spend more time with his children than his father had spent with him. But

~ ~

when Ken's job came to a screeching halt, the children were
not a source of comfort. Ken had a heart attack, and while
in intensive care, he was forced to face himself. He felt
alone and isolated, defeated and unsure of how to deal with
his life. This incredibly gifted man was a far cry from being
the pillar of strength he had portrayed all his adult life. He
was out of touch with his internal pain, and this lack of
understanding made him incapable of overcoming his
problems.

His past had not taught him to take care of internal
needs. He was not equipped to search inside himself for the
resources to rebuild his world. But with help from his wife
and with a stretch of counseling, he finally learned to get in
touch with his inner self.

How Women Are Socialized

Women face barriers that make it difficult to obtain
and maintain the internal balance necessary for being
effective. These barriers are different from those experienced by most men because society socializes women and
men in different ways.

Women's roles and identities have always been
attached to others; nurturing others, emotionally supporting
others and generally taking care of others. These are
commendable qualities as long as they don't compromise
the individual's self-worth. If care-giving women are appreciated, respected, and rewarded, their lives can be meaningful. But a woman's chances of feeling good about herself
decrease when she gives out of obligation rather than out of
choice.

If women don't accept their own needs as important,
they won't be able to see themselves as important; they will

perceive their roles only as satisfiers of other people's needs.

Unfortunately, many women buy into these generational messages of gender bias and prejudice. They often experience themselves as next to nothing without others, and, all too often, consider themselves important only in their roles as someone else's daughter, spouse, lover or mother. So when their children leave the nest or when the nest is upset by divorce or death, women often feel lost and without purpose.

For generations, women have experienced internal conflict about their identities, but in recent years, the conflict has flared. As women began to recognize their right to have choices in their lives, they also inherited the battle of proving their worth in the workplace.

Messages of Inferiority

Religion has been a source of the messages of inferiority for young girls. Their God, their higher power, is typically male, referred to in most of the world as "Father," and not likely to be forgiving and non-punishing. Instead, he is a man to fear. Judeo-Christian, Islamic and some Eastern religions also teach women to be submissive to men, to "love, honor, and obey."

Women who were physically, sexually or emotionally abused feel inferior in another way. Unconsciously, they often feel shame or accept the blame for the abuse and continue on in life feeling lesser or blaming themselves for things that are not their fault.

Women in general were socialized in their families, cultures and society to accept an inferior role. The classic fairy tales are still with us to remind us that men either save women or conquer them. But women can no longer accept

~ ~

these myths and the resulting restrictive bonds; they must overcome these destructive messages before they can develop Self-Love and Self-Power.

Role Models

Mothers are one of the strongest models of behavior, beliefs and attitudes for their daughters. But these mothers, as children, often were subjected to the same or similar myths. They too were affected by their own histories, histories that seldom focused on the need for independence and taking charge of their own lives, histories that were slanted toward the myth that women had to be taken care of, had to be non-assertive, had to be unchallenged.

Perception of Control

Many women see themselves as having less control than men over the outcome of their behavior. Because of the way women have been "enculturated," they have less self-confidence than men, especially in male-oriented activities. When they are successful in such activities, they often believe their success is due to luck or an especially easy task.

Men, on the other hand, attribute success to their own skills, their own talents or efforts, regardless of the task. Ironically, failure is a completely different story. Women are quick to attribute failure to themselves, to a lack of skill, talent or effort. Men place the blame on others, bad luck or the difficulty of the task.

A pattern of self-blame contributes to negative self-image and many women become convinced that they're incapable of changing things in their present lives or in their futures. Researchers describe these behavior patterns as either external or internal attributions. When women are successful, they tend to credit others; when men are successful, they tend to credit themselves. When women fail, they tend to blame themselves; when men fail, they tend to blame others.

These differences have enormous implications for how women perceive the control they have over their lives. Because they are socialized to depend on and defer to others, they often have a poor sense of control. They are not as convinced as men that they can effect necessary change and most cultures reinforce this conviction. At work, they often wait for promotions and raises rather than asking for them. In their personal lives, when relationships go wrong, they may wait too long before they take action on their own, hoping the man or circumstance will change.

In some cultures, women are granted a position of power over the home, but this power is "given" to them only because it serves the needs of other family members. Therefore, even this power has an external source.

Mixed Messages

Women raised in the period just before the beginning of the Women's Movement were socialized traditionally as children but non-traditionally as adults. As children, they learned that a woman's place was only in the home. As adults, they are learning that a woman's place is wherever she wants it to be.

Women caught in this transition were once led to believe that caring for others was most important. Now they are being told that it's just as important to care for themselves. Women growing up after the beginning of the

Women's Movement may have been raised more non-traditionally as children, but they still face a world consisting of a majority who hold traditional views.

These mixed messages create vague feelings of failure for women, both in finding their acceptable roles and in pleasing those with different views. To promote positive growth and energy, they need to find an acceptable balance between each of their needs.

Half of society sees a career role for women as positive; and the other half sees it as negative. The same is true for the traditional homemaker role. This lack of consensus, even among women, makes either choice feel like a no-win situation.

In recent years, we've seen more than a glimmer of light to guide women along a path toward balance. The needed light radiates through women who believe in themselves and who have taken responsibility for the quality of their lives. It also radiates through men who are secure enough within themselves to recognize women as equals.

More women than ever now recognize that they don't have to make an either/or choice; they can choose both, or a portion of both, and both dreams can become their reality.

The GEM model makes women more effective by showing them how to recognize and accept their unique identities. It creates a model of effectiveness from a female perspective, rather than trying to emulate the masculine model of effectiveness.

A Sense of Confusion and Failure

Joan was thirty-eight. She was intelligent, hardworking and determined. She had worked on and off throughout her twelve-year marriage. Her husband traveled

~ ~

frequently, and her two children, ages six and ten, were becoming less dependent upon her. She had always dreamed about owning her own company, but had never pushed herself to make it happen.

She decided to go for counseling, although she wasn't exactly sure what she hoped to accomplish. As she put it, "I'm not sure what's really bugging me."

For Joan, the previous two years had been uneventful. She insisted that she had decided to put her dream on the back burner only because of her husband's absence from the home. She said she resented him because of it, even though their lifestyle depended on his income. The more she discussed what she wasn't doing in her life, the more she blamed her husband. She explained that she had worked to help supplement their income while he was finishing college and she didn't feel she was getting the same support in return.

Looking back through this young woman's past and working through the GEM needs, we discovered that Joan's mother had been a career woman. She had encouraged Joan to go to college and seek a degree in business management. Joan had loved her courses and had done well. Her first job held great promise, but she had given up the job to become a full-time wife. When asked if this had been her choice, she admitted with some hesitation and confusion that it had been.

She also expressed her opinion that "my father left my mother while I was in college, and although my mother disagrees, I'm sure he left because of my mother's career."

After struggling with why she had come to this conclusion about the divorce, Joan said, "I believe it came from the fact that, over and over, my father spoke to me about how important it was to be there for your husband."

Exploring the GEM needs more deeply, Joan realized that it was her view of her parents' divorce that had stopped her from becoming the effective woman she was capable of being.

Her deepest fear was attaining her own personal success and losing her husband in the process. Learning to overcome this fear and learning that her relationship with her husband was different from that of her parents allowed Joan to pursue what she wanted. When she no longer blamed her husband for her dependency, she was able to take control of her own decisions.

An Opportunity to Change

The GEM model offered both Joan and Ken the opportunity to confront parts of themselves that they had ignored and to make the necessary changes to achieve balance. During our lifetimes, hidden messages and misinterpretations about ourselves and others have shaped our relationships and our decisions. Let's expose these untruths to the light and create new truths that will allow us to live freer, more effective lives.

Chapter Four

Assessing Your GEM Balance

~ ~

Are your internal needs in balance? Probably not. But what is that supposed to mean?

No person is in perfect balance in all three GEM relationships. Some people are in perfect balance in one of the three relationships. A few are fortunate enough to be in balance in two, but most people need help in all three of the relationship categories.

What do we mean by being in balance? Technically, that you should internally possess equal amounts of Self-Love and Self-Power characteristics, no more, no less. You also should possess equal amounts of the other two pairs of GEM relationship needs.

The Test

To assess your areas of balance or imbalance, I have developed a test I call the "Personality Dimension Scale." It

~ ~

measures to what degree you operate out of each of the six needs that are critical for effective living. Before using it in this book, I tested several hundred men and women, using a broad sample encompassing a wide range of ages, socio-economic classes, races and occupational categories and levels.

Prepare yourself for this test by taking a few minutes to read the instructions before answering the questions, and be sure to answer the questions honestly and from the heart. Give only the answer that truly reflects how you personally feel. If you're unsure, pick the answer closest to your feelings.

There's no time limit to the test. Take whatever time you need.

Instructions: Listed below are thirty statements that describe peoples' attitudes and beliefs. We would like to know how you personally feel about these statements. Please read each statement carefully, then check the space beside the answer which best represents your degree of agreement or disagreement with each statement:

1. I am proud of my ethics, values and conduct most of the time.
___ Strongly Agree   ___ Agree
___ Disagree   ___ Strongly Disagree

2. I believe in my own talent and my ability to enhance and develop myself.
___ Strongly Agree   ___ Agree
___ Disagree   ___ Strongly Disagree

3. I wish friends wouldn't be so quick to hug and kiss me when they say hello. I'm often quite uncomfortable touching and being touched by other people.
___ Strongly Agree   ___ Agree
___ Disagree   ___ Strongly Disagree

4. I don't care whether I "belong" or not.
___ Strongly Agree   ___ Agree
___ Disagree   ___ Strongly Disagree

5. I have a lot to offer at work and in my home, and I expect to be acknowledged.
___ Strongly Agree   ___ Agree
___ Disagree   ___ Strongly Disagree

6. Getting people to do the right thing depends upon ability. Luck has little or nothing to do with it.
___ Strongly Agree   ___ Agree
___ Disagree   ___ Strongly Disagree

7. It's not important to try to manipulate those around me to see things my way.
___ Strongly Agree   ___ Agree
___ Disagree   ___ Strongly Disagree

8. If I become angry with my partner, I don't normally feel free to show my feelings.
___ Strongly Agree   ___ Agree
___ Disagree   ___ Strongly Disagree

~ ~

9. Quite often when I have problems I don't seem to have the inner strength to stand alone and I wish I had others to lean on.

_____ Strongly Agree   _____ Agree
_____ Disagree   _____ Strongly Disagree

10. I have the capacity to be totally honest about myself and I'm not afraid to disclose my weaknesses to my friends and loved ones.

_____ Strongly Agree   _____ Agree
_____ Disagree   _____ Strongly Disagree

11. Much of the time I believe that I am NOT responsible for my troubles.

_____ Strongly Agree   _____ Agree
_____ Disagree   _____ Strongly Disagree

12. I really believe that most people I know don't look up to me and don't respect me.

_____ Strongly Agree   _____ Agree
_____ Disagree   _____ Strongly Disagree

13. It would please me greatly to have children just like me.

_____ Strongly Agree   _____ Agree
_____ Disagree   _____ Strongly Disagree

14. You make your own luck.

_____ Strongly Agree   _____ Agree
_____ Disagree   _____ Strongly Disagree

~ ~

15. In a loving relationship, I have enough trust in myself and my partner to maintain a deep and open level of communication.

___ Strongly Agree ___ Agree
___ Disagree ___ Strongly Disagree

16. I am an independent human being and derive a good deal of inner satisfaction and peace when I am alone.

___ Strongly Agree ___ Agree
___ Disagree ___ Strongly Disagree

17. I'm convinced that I am unique and that my contribution in life is valuable and important to myself and others.

___ Strongly Agree ___ Agree
___ Disagree ___ Strongly Disagree

18. I strive to gain control over the events around me at work and in my social life.

___ Strongly Agree ___ Agree
___ Disagree ___ Strongly Disagree

19. The best leaders are those who see what others need or want and who work to make that happen.

___ Strongly Agree ___ Agree
___ Disagree ___ Strongly Disagree

20. Even though others may have strengths I don't possess, I consider myself of equal value as a human being.

___ Strongly Agree ___ Agree
___ Disagree ___ Strongly Disagree

~ ~

21. I feel I have only myself to count on, but that's okay.

___ Strongly Agree   ___ Agree
___ Disagree   ___ Strongly Disagree

22. I am afraid to make myself vulnerable to someone I like very much.

___ Strongly Agree   ___ Agree
___ Disagree   ___ Strongly Disagree

23. A person who is able and willing to work hard has a good chance of succeeding in whatever he/she wants to do.

___ Strongly Agree   ___ Agree
___ Disagree   ___ Strongly Disagree

24. I often have the feeling that I can do nearly everything well.

___ Strongly Agree   ___ Agree
___ Disagree   ___ Strongly Disagree

25. I feel that I'm a person of worth, at least on an equal basis with others.

___ Strongly Agree   ___ Agree
___ Disagree   ___ Strongly Disagree

26. I have choices available and can create personal change through my own efforts.

___ Strongly Agree   ___ Agree
___ Disagree   ___ Strongly Disagree

27. It pleases me when people share their feelings with me.
___ Strongly Agree   ___ Agree
___ Disagree   ___ Strongly Disagree

28. Adversity has taught me how strong I am.
___ Strongly Agree   ___ Agree
___ Disagree   ___ Strongly Disagree

29. I have left a good mark on the world and some people in it.
___ Strongly Agree   ___ Agree
___ Disagree   ___ Strongly Disagree

30. I enjoy exercising my power as a person who creates positive change and controls events taking place around me.
___ Strongly Agree   ___ Agree
___ Disagree   ___ Strongly Disagree

"Scoring" Key for Personality Dimension Scale
Step 1:
On questions 3, 7, 8, 9, 11, 12 and 22, score
   1 for Strongly Agree,
   2 for Agree,
   3 for Disagree, and
   4 for Strongly Disagree.
Step 2:
For all other questions, score
   4 for Strongly Agree,
   3 for Agree,
   2 for Disagree
   1 for Strongly Disagree.

~ ~

Step 3:

Using the chart below, fill in the blanks with the number you entered for the 30 questions. Add your scores for each group and enter the numbers on the "Total" line.

A. Self-Love
1._____12._____13._____24._____25._____
Total____

B. Self-Power
2._____11._____14._____23._____26._____
Total____

C. Intimacy
3._____10._____15._____22._____27._____
Total____

D. Solitude
4._____9._____16._____21._____28._____
Total____

E. Equality
5._____8._____17._____20._____29._____
Total____

F. Manipulation
6._____7._____18._____19._____30._____
Total____

Step 4:
Fill in your totals in the corresponding blanks below.
Step 5:
To determine the balance between each of the three

~ ~

groups of personality dimensions below, subtract the LOWER score from the HIGHER score in each group, and place your answer on the "Balance Score" line. Then identify the name of the dimension with the HIGHEST SCORE.

EXAMPLE:

A. Self-Love Total = *10*

B. Self-Power Total = *12*

Balance Score = *2*

Name of Highest Dimension: *Self-Power*

A. Self-Love Total = _____

B. Self-Power Total = _____

Balance Score (subtract) = _____

Name of Highest Dimension: _____

C. Intimacy Total = _____

D. Solitude Total = _____

Balance Score (subtract) = _____

Name of Highest Dimension: _____

E. Equality Total = _____

F. Manipulation Total = _____

Balance Score (subtract) = _____

Name of Highest Dimension: _____

~ ~

Recognizing Your Need Imbalances

If your score for any need was exactly the same as its
partner need, you ended up with a balance score of "0."
That is a perfect balance. If the difference between the
need dimension scores was "1" that also is considered *in
balance.*

If your balance score showed a difference of "2" or
more in either dimension, your needs are out of balance and
you should work to get them back into balance. The higher
the balance score, the more out of balance you are. A score
of "4" or more indicates a serious imbalance.

Visualizing Your Balance

It might help you to visualize how close or far away
you are from balance in each of the three important need
relationships.

In the three pairs of circles below, notice that each pair
overlaps a little. The overlap is shaded. Inside each pair of
circles, you will find a straight line scale marked with a "0"
in the center of the overlap and other numbers ranging from
"1" to "4" to the left and right of the center. As you can see,
a score of 1 is just on the edge of the overlap in both directions and is still considered "in balance."

To visualize your score, find the numeric balance you
marked down for the three pairs of relationships in Step 4 of
the scoring key. Then plot each of your three balance scores
in the appropriate set of circles.

Example: If your Self-Love/Self-Power balance score
was "0," place an "X" on the line in the middle of the
overlap between the two relevant circles. However, if your
score was "2" and your highest dimension was Self-Love,

~ ~

put your "X" on the line where it is marked "2" in the left-hand circle designated "Self-Love." Follow these instructions for each of the three circles.

When you have finished, you will see graphically how you stand in each relationship compared to how you would stand if you were in perfect, or reasonably good, balance.

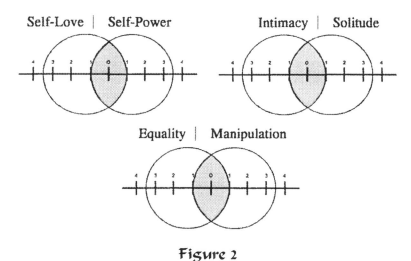

Figure 2

Determining the Strength of Your Six Needs

Average Scores: To determine whether your score is high, medium or low in each of the three needs, compare your scores to the following norms established by our initial testing of the Personality Dimension Scale:

	Self-Love	*Self-Power*
High	17.3-20.0	17.5-20.0
Medium	15.2-17.2	15.4-17.4
Low	15.1 or less	15.3 or less

	Intimacy	*Solitude*
High	16.5-20.0	14.9-20.0
Medium	14.4-16.4	12.8-14.8
Low	14.3 or less	12.7 or less

	Equality	*Manipulation*
High	17.8-20.0	16.1-20.0
Medium	15.7-17.7	14.0-16.0
Low	15.6 or less	13.9 or less

It is important to remember that you would want your score to be as high as possible in each need. Even though your scores for two needs may be in balance, you may be so low in both that you're not as effective as you might be. For example, if you scored "10" in Self-Love and "10" in Self-Power, your needs were in balance. But it also shows that you probably don't like yourself very much and have very little self confidence. Under those circumstances, we could predict that you will face many problems that will block your effectiveness.

Ideally, you would want to have high, balanced scores. If you are not as high as you'd like to be in one or more of the needs, there is a series of action steps you can take to improve your area(s) of weakness. We will explore these steps in chapters to come.

Traits of People with Ideal Balance

Men and women whose needs are in balance have rich and effective lives. They realize and accept where they are in life and take full responsibility for their choices and decisions.

~ ~

Some people live long lives but get stuck emotionally, remaining as children or teenagers, never becoming effective adults. But others who are internally balanced or reasonably close to it look forward to moving from one stage of life to another. They learn, they grow and they challenge each change. They develop themselves and experience their full potential.

Being in balance means that we have objective perspective and that we are psychologically anchored. That doesn't mean we can't move. On the contrary, it means we become freer because we know who we are. As we learn, our self-knowledge is updated and we change accordingly.

People in balance are better able to make change gracefully and without fear. They understand that change is inevitable.

Abraham Maslow, a world-famous psychologist, labeled this type of need balance "self-actualization." He found that self-actualization is characterized by the following traits:

Spontaneity.

Problem-centeredness.

A need for occasional solitude and privacy.

A freshness of perception.

An attraction for the unfamiliar, the new, and the unexpected.

A sense of unity with nature and all humankind.

A related feeling of belonging to all humankind, a sense of the interrelationship of all people.

A tendency to relate to other persons as individuals and not to be influenced by prejudicial factors such as race, religion or group membership.

A firm sense of one's own ethics.

Creativity.

~ ~

Resistance to the influence of one's own culture
    when that influence conflicts with personal
    standards.

You are now ready to open the door to *your* "self-actualization."

Chapter Five

Self-Love/Self-Power Relationship: Issues

~ ~

I've spent many years exploring the human need to obtain Self-Love and Self-Power. And I examined how our need for love and power impacts our lives in significant ways. But not until I began looking at the negative impact that gender bias and other prejudices have on a person's attitudes and behavior, did I begin to thoroughly understand how our love for self and others is severely compromised when we operate with judgmental attitudes and beliefs.

As I personally became conscious of some of my own not-so-obvious biases and prejudices, I began confronting them through a process of honest self-disclosure, journal keeping, and discussions with people I respect and trust.

I urge you to discuss this chapter with someone of the opposite sex as well as some one of the same sex, persons you respect and know to be objective. Open discussions can help you better understand the different perspectives men and women have and how they go about the business of gaining greater insights into themselves and others.

There is no right or wrong way to explore one's identity. But it's impossible to fully understand yourself without first understanding the different types of love and power that exist, and acknowledging how your need for Self-Love and Self-Power affects your total behavior. So move through this chapter concentrating on your need to love yourself. You should pay attention to whatever mental pictures, thoughts or inner feelings pop into your conscious awareness. There is always new information for you to discover about yourself, about who you are and why you think and feel as you do. These new insights will prove invaluable when dealing with persons whose perceptions and perspectives differ from yours. Learning to love yourself in ways that make you more sensitive and understanding of others is especially helpful for communicating your own ideas and feelings. Before going on, visualize these needs and take another look at the definitions below:

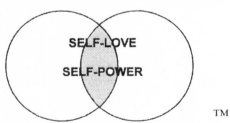

Self-Love: a liking for, and satisfaction with yourself; a sense of self-value, self-respect and self-appreciation.

Self-Power: a belief in your own abilities and the skills to develop yourself; it is the capacity to enlarge your range of choices, which creates personal change.

Nothing is more critical for achieving personal satisfaction, success and effectiveness than recognizing and acknowledging your personal need for Self-Love. It's not always easy to reach deep inside for this experience of loving yourself because it often causes painful issues to surface. This "inside" work can only be done by you, but the rewards are endless if you go about it in a thoughtful and gentle way.

It is through Self-Love that you'll learn and grow from the difficulties that come your way, developing more resources for healing the internal pain that would otherwise go unattended, leaving you "stuck" in out-dated and self-punitive attitudes or behavior.

Self-Love is a feeling about yourself that, when balanced with your need for Self-Power, promotes personal success. It's that internalized feeling of "okayness" and calm about yourself, an internal calm that acts as a stabilizer in the face of emotional, mental, physical or financial crises. When we're not grounded, our lives can spin out of control. Take the example of Fred and Jane.

A Couple Out of Control

Fred was blessed with social ease. His enthusiasm and energy were contagious and made him easy to like. His status in the community coupled with his material gains spoke of his success. Yet, Fred quietly suffered severe bouts of depression. When he wasn't depressed, he often had raging temper tantrums. His wife, Jane, appeared outgoing and easy. For the most part, she cared for her family adequately and in an appropriate manner. However, Jane too suffered. She secretly numbed herself with alcohol and prescription drugs.

Fred and Jane had three children, all of whom displayed types of behavior that suggested emotional turmoil in their own lives. The family resided in a "desirable" neighborhood, the children attended private schools; they were a family who, from the outside, appeared to have it all.

Their symptoms and behavior contradicted the picture they presented to the outside world. Jane's addictions and Fred's depression and unpredictable rages point to the fact that neither Jane nor Fred was aware of the importance of developing and satisfying her/his individual need for Self-Love.

We often overlook this human need because we're taught early in life that we're not worthy of such wonderful feelings as Self-Love or self-appreciation. As adults we don't accept that *we* are in charge of how, when and to what degree we experience these good feelings. Fred's and Jane's solution for solving their personal unhappiness and discontentment was to "run away" and avoid their need to deal with their feelings and thoughts. They weren't connecting with their Self-Love and the internal strength that it creates. By anesthetizing themselves they "avoided" their own issues and were unconscious of their children's problems. It took a suicide attempt by one of the children for Jane, at least, to seek help for herself and her family.

Biases and Prejudices Attached to Self-Love

When we are very young, we form beliefs and attitudes about ourselves and others. These beliefs and attitudes color our way of thinking and affect our style of communication.

We'd like to think that every belief we possess is totally our own, that we deliberately planted it inside ourselves and that our belief system is unique to us.

However, from the moment we're born, we start with beliefs and attitudes given to us by others. Little by little, we pick up ideas about what's right or wrong, who's good or bad. Some of our mothers and fathers told us we were talented and wonderful, and we believed them. Others of us were told that we were rotten or stupid or would never amount to anything, and we grew up feeling that way.

We learned ideas about other people, other races, other religions, other customs. We listened to what people told us about the proper roles for girls, for boys, for women and for men. It's nearly impossible to grow up in a family or culture without accepting many of the ideas and opinions that we heard our parents or other role models express over the years.

Their biases and prejudices often become ours. These biases and prejudices (and any other differences) play themselves out in our day-to-day lives. They influence our behavior and affect our picture of the world. Far too often, they create the stereotypes that limit our involvement with those who are different from us, restricting our experience of ourselves and of others, limiting our personal growth and success.

To become aware of your personal biases and prejudices, you must take a step into your past where the messages you received about men and women, different cultures, ethnic groups, races or others who represent something different from yourself reside. This part of your journey, while informative, can also be uncomfortable. As you begin recognizing the biases and prejudices that make up a part of your belief system, you need to begin questioning the realities of your beliefs.

~ ~

Men and Gender Biases Attached to Self-Love

Some people are convinced that men know how to direct their love only to the outside world, that a man's love for his spouse, his children or his significant other and how he provides for them determine how "successful" he is. But Self-Love is not something men are encouraged to think about. Warm feelings are generated outwardly but rarely stored inside as a reservoir to draw upon when needed. Men are not encouraged to think of such things or to understand the significance and correlation between their development of Self-Love and their success.

Many men buy into this bias, and in so doing, find they can't experience self-worth except in terms of how society or strangers view them. This robs them of the opportunity to express their deeper needs and to feel comfortable about nurturing themselves.

Moving further and further away from their emotions and the more loving aspects of their personalities, they lose touch with their warmer sides and erect barriers that distance them from others. Their behavior becomes superficial and negates the pleasurable feelings that come out of Self-Love.

This less than warm behavior prompts some women to perceive men as uncaring and to look to them mostly as a means of financial support. Men resent this perception, complaining that they're only meal tickets for their mates and families. Yet they don't seem to be able to break the bonds of the bias.

During midlife, this resentment can turn into anger, building up inside to create internal conflict. They continue distancing themselves as they learned long ago; they perpetuate their inability to express their inner feelings.

Hank and Self-Love

Hank loves sports, especially those he can play with his buddies. On Sunday afternoons he and his buddies get together for their weekly game of basketball at a local outdoor court. "It's a great time for me," he told me, "because I give it my all for a couple of hours and get rid of my pent up frustrations. I don't have to think about anything but getting around the guy in front of me and scoring the basket. After the game, we sit around joking and kidding each other. You know, nothing really serious. It feels so good just to be able to talk without having to think first. When my wife and I hang out together, talking is always a big deal. You know, heavy. She's always asking me how I *feel* about something. That's okay, I guess, but you can only take so much of that."

Typically, Hank accepts a bias that suppresses his deeper feelings, so that shifting from non-personal conversation to a deeper expression of himself is uncomfortable. Both forms of communication have their place and meet specific needs, but a bias such as the one Hank carries makes it impossible for him to communicate his emotional needs even to himself.

Women and Gender Biases Attached to Self-Love

Until recently, women were taught that Self-Love depends on others. They learned to identify themselves as daughters, as sweethearts, as wives and as mothers. The message they received as children was that, if they love other people, their love will be returned, and when it is, they will feel good about themselves. So women learned to attach their love to other people rather than to themselves. Because a major goal for women is to find and then maintain loving relationships with others, their sense of self becomes attached to and structured around others. If some disruption occurs in that love, women tend to see it not just as a loss of a relationship, but as something resembling a total loss of self.

Times are changing, however, and more women are learning to identify themselves as independent persons. Yet many women still unconsciously cling to the old biases which create a lack of internal self-confidence and diminish feelings of self-worth. When that happens, women often blame others for their unhappiness. So even though men do have difficulty experiencing Self-Love, gender biases deposit far more positive self-worth messages into their subconscious minds than is the case with women. This is not surprising, since society appears to value men more than women.

While women find it much easier than men to be in touch with their self-worth reservoirs, they have smaller reservoirs from which to draw. Studies show that starting in late elementary school, males score much higher in self-worth than females. During adolescence, girls receive conflicting messages about achievement and popularity, and they start doubting themselves. Although scientists disagree as to why this happens, self-worth differences continue during high school and college years. Perhaps scientists should examine the hidden messages about women that are played out through bias and prejudice as a way to determine why women have less self-worth than men. They should consider how girls are treated in the classroom: ignored, overlooked and made to feel inferior to the boys. Because of gender bias, men also have higher expectations and higher aspirations than women, so their self-confidence levels are higher than women's throughout the adult years. Many young girls accept and internalize negative messages about themselves to a greater degree than boys. They are taught to be more aware of feelings. Therefore, their internalization process is more susceptible to all types of information, positive and *negative.* Their awareness antennae are more alert. Boys are not tuned in the same way and appear to be less damaged by what's going on around them.

Karen's Lack of Self-Love

Karen, thirty-two, a bank vice-president, grew up with an abusive stepparent, which affected her capacity for Self-Love. "From the ages of seven to seventeen," she says, "I was constantly criticized and belittled by my stepfather. If he wasn't making a joke about me, he was angry with me. When I brought home a "B" instead of an "A," I was told it wasn't good enough and that I should have tried harder.

Instead of building my self-esteem, my stepfather verbally humiliated me. Now, as an adult, I find that I'm never satisfied with myself. I'm constantly trying to be perfect, and it's driving me and my family crazy." Karen couldn't figure out why she was the only one affected by her stepfather. "I have two brothers, one older and one younger. The three of us are all pretty close in age, yet, when we talk about the times when we were kids, I sometimes feel like I came from another family. Neither one of my brothers remembers being humiliated by our stepfather. Even though they didn't like him, they were able to let his nasty behavior roll off their backs."

Steve's Conflict

Steve, forty-two, came into counseling because his wife was talking about divorce. This was Steve's second marriage and he wanted to keep it. He felt he deeply loved his wife and was frightened at the thought of losing her.

She had begged him for more than a year to join her in therapy. He resisted because he had been raised to believe that a "real" man should be strong and capable of handling his own affairs and making his own decisions. Steve's cultural background reinforced this message with its built-in beliefs about men being the heads of their households and making the major decisions for their families.

According to Steve's family history, his culture and society, his wife was breaking the rules by not accepting the money he provided as proof of his love for her. Steve thought of himself as a "modern man" and did not object to his wife entering counseling. "After all," he said, "women want to talk about 'everything' and need this type of support." Steve's understanding of his wife's need for counseling was based on his bias about the emotional needs of women.

Entering counseling was difficult for Steve, but the threat of his marriage ending overruled his biases. He didn't like to talk about himself and was especially turned off at the idea of exploring his past to understand how his biases were part of his present problem. In his mind, he was there to convince the therapist that his wife needed to understand how good she had it and to quit making unreasonable demands.

This man was in a "Catch 22" situation. He was deeply affected by his wife's thoughts about leaving. Yet his attitude and behavior did not reflect his fears or his sincere love. Shortly after Steve started counseling, his father died unexpectedly. Steve was overwhelmed with his loss. His wife, encultured to take care of others, put her need to leave the marriage on hold. "After all," she told the therapist, "isn't it my job to offer support at a time like this?" She decided to stay, but the real problem didn't change. Steve did, what, for a man, in this situation is often predictable. He avoided getting in touch with his subconscious emotions. His only way of coping was to push his sadness away and throw himself into his work. Steve was not sure how to mourn. He thought he should just get on with living and take care of the business at hand.

Although his wife had made the choice to be there for Steve, she once again saw him as cold and distant, making it impossible for her to reach out and comfort him. Neither Steve nor his wife was able to talk about the pain of losing a loved one. They lost the opportunity to share in the healing that can create a stronger bond of friendship. Steve's bias about love, about women and about his own emotions had once again gotten in his way of understanding Self-Love. His wife's biases about Self-Love, her conviction that love was something attached to others, left her feeling resentful about her decision to stay.

Counseling and commitment opened the door for them jointly to confront their biases and to re-address how gender biases were affecting their ability to love themselves and each other. Their marriage did not have to end. It simply had to grow in a new direction, free from biases and cultural beliefs that interfered with each individual's responsibility to get beyond the old stereotyping. Their marriage began

again when they found a new way to communicate their
needs and love to one another.

Body Image

Our perceptions of our bodies often affect our sense of
Self-Love. Unfortunately, few women or men are satisfied
with their bodies. Most of us see every blemish, no matter
how minute, as a reason for self-dissatisfaction. Being short
or tall, overweight or underweight, large or small-breasted
can cause self-doubt. Even though the blemish may be seen
only by its owner, it can cause years of agonizing self-
consciousness.

Women tend to evaluate their bodies by how they
compare to magazine or television ads and by how sexually
attractive they feel. Men learn to appraise their own bodies
competitively. Their sense of self-worth depends on how
athletic, well-coordinated, long-enduring, responsive and
sexually active they are.

Both men and women rely too heavily on Madison
Avenue image-makers for a sense of self-worth and Self-
Love. They fail to accept that bodies vary and that the
variety is what makes us unique and special. Bodies of
every shape were the subjects of world-famous artists:
Modigliani, Renoir, Rubens, Picasso. Each admired and
painted a very different type.

Cosmetic surgeons make their living treating people
with poor body images. Some patients, of course, have
serious deformities, but most are normal in the sense that
what they perceive as "wrong" and want fixed may not be
visible to anyone but themselves. Most men hate being bald.
To them, going bald is a sign of declining attractiveness,
diminished masculinity and the beginning of old age. But

nationwide surveys of women report that women are attracted to bald men because to them it's a symbol of strength and masculinity.

Many women agonize over their stretch marks or the loss of muscle tone. But men repeatedly report that they are oblivious to these imperfections when they are with someone they care about and whose company they enjoy.

More women than men elect to change their faces or bodies through cosmetic surgery, but the number of male patients is dramatically increasing, even with formerly female-dominated procedures such as face lifts and nose-straightening. Men and women alike, if they're not careful, can become victims of unrealistic ideals and expectations when they fail to meet their needs for Self-Love.

Loving Yourself

Self-Love is the strongest internal resource for building self-worth. It enables you to turn inward for comfort and peacefulness. This is where you can discover all that you are, all that you're about and all that you can become — your personal truths! Knowing and believing that you have the ability to change your truths and create new truths is the power that comes from loving yourself.

Developing a healthy love for yourself is your first step toward effective living. Challenge yourself to take the risk of looking inward to find all that is positive in yourself and to eliminate any negative internal emotions, thoughts, or feelings that are standing in the way of your Self-Love.

Fears, jealousies, and envy are your internal enemies. They chip away at your self-worth by producing negative pictures that cloud your ability to perceive yourself, other people or situations correctly. This stops you from trusting your own judgment and places roadblocks in the path of your potential. Satisfying your internal need for Self-Love is your protection against these enemies.

Liking Yourself

Liking yourself is another aspect of Self-Love. It lets you be your own best friend. Have you ever given any thought to the amount of consideration, respect, forgiveness, love and gentleness you are willing to give to others? Giving this same amount of caring to yourself will ensure the enhancement of your self-worth. Evidence from research and clinical observation shows that effective people think well of themselves. Some people carry it to extremes, of course. There's a big difference between the braggart and the effective person who has a quiet sense of personal worth.

A Woman Who Lacked Self-Love

Janice, forty-one, had been divorced for seven years. She had a seventeen-year-old son whom she had raised alone since her divorce. At first, she wanted counseling because she felt depressed. She complained about loss of appetite and an inability to sleep well.

She said she was "always on the brink of crying." She felt that her son no longer needed her and that her life was empty. "The last seven years have been the pits. I don't have any close friends, my relationships with men are lousy, and my social life is zero."

As time went on, Janice told a familiar story. She was reared in a home where her parents believed that children were to be seen but not heard. Although she did well in school, she didn't do as well as her older brother, who was considered a genius. She believed him to be the favorite child.

Her mother taught her that it was vain and selfish to pamper or love herself. She told Janice that her interest in boys was silly and that her friends were only interested in her because they could take advantage of her. Janice began to believe this and, eventually, withdrew into herself.

She had worked as an accountant for the same firm since graduating from college. And although she wasn't particularly happy with her job, she chose to stay because "it pays well, I'm my own boss and no one bothers me."

Janice was in a rut. She didn't like, let alone love, herself. In spite of her competence, her caring qualities and her attractiveness, she felt lonely, insecure and dissatisfied with her life.

Janice needed to confront the old messages of her past and learn to see herself in a new way that was positive and loving. She needed to recognize that what she had learned in her family about herself and the outside world had not been totally accurate.

Learning about the importance of Self-Love helped Janice understand the need for change. Janice faced hard personal work in her pursuit of a happier life. But her decision to acknowledge and use her competence and good common sense to challenge her past and to create pleasure in her life was both adventurous and exciting.

Acknowledging her ability to love her son in a way that taught him to believe in himself and to stand on his own helped Janice to use this same ability to love herself. By questioning her past, she discovered that her mother had lived a sheltered and deprived life, always fearful of people and their intentions. This new insight into her mother gave

~ ~

Janice more understanding of her own discomforts. With this new awareness came the courage for Janice to reach out to others.

Realizing that socializing was not exclusive to men, she got involved in activities outside her home. These interests introduced Janice to a larger world with different people in it and different messages about herself.

Slowly, she began to feel self-assured and content. Best of all, her depression lifted. Learning the importance of Self-Love let Janice experience good feelings she had never known.

Humor

Humor is another positive gain that comes out of Self-Love. The ability to laugh at ourselves can lighten our lives. Liking yourself lets you feel confident and satisfied with who you are and eliminates the need to be self-critical.

A keynote speaker was addressing a large and impressive audience at an important conference. She was quite short and had been standing on a box so she could see her audience over the top of the podium. To make a point, she tried to move away from the podium, but misjudged her step, taking a not-so-glamorous tumble. She landed on her feet, but not before going through some fancy gymnastics that were anything but graceful. As she caught herself, she burst out laughing. The fact that she could laugh at herself helped her "land on her feet" with her audience. She could return to the podium and make her audience comfortable enough to laugh with her.

Her topic that day was the differences between men and women in the 90's, their gender biases and changing roles. "This definitely was not a gender issue or a condition of the 90's, she told the audience. "I simply was born a klutz." Her humor eased her audience and endeared her to them.

Had she not felt love for herself, this experience could have left her embarrassed and unnerved, and the rest of the program would have been downhill.

We always recover best when we know how to laugh.

Keeping in Touch

Self-Love is a navigator for your emotions. Being in touch with what you are feeling and why you are feeling it will help you better understand your motives and your behavior.

You cannot change things unless you're aware change is needed. So if there is something you do not love or like about yourself, be willing to journey back to your past to find the negative messages that diminish your Self-Love. Being conscious of and accepting your weaknesses as well as your strengths will give you the permission to make mistakes, all of which are part of Self-Love. Nothing is better than a good mistake to help you on your way to success, providing you learn from that mistake.

The Self-Power Need

Self-Power is the key to your potential. It's a place within you that is strong and gives you the courage to discover your own talents. Possessing Self-Power frees you from self-doubt and enhances your self-esteem.

Most internal needs cannot be fulfilled until you are willing to take charge of your own life. Self-Power is no exception. Once you have experienced the positive energy

~ ~

and control created by meeting your need for Self-Power, you will begin to understand its value in your life.

Can you remember a time when your body and mind were in tune with one another? You felt great about yourself! Deep inside you had a feeling of contentment and happiness. You were able to let your creative self take over exploring your talents and trusting your own judgments. You believed in yourself. These are the times when your Self-Power is operating and you feel confident in taking the good risks in life, risks that allow you to experience your effectiveness, your personal success and your unlimited potential.

Different Types of Power

People often think that power comes only through acclaim, financial success or position. These only represent your power in the outside world, they cannot protect you from the inequities of life.

Having an effect on your environment is another type of power that is closely connected to Self-Power but is a little different. "Fighting City Hall" or getting together with neighbors to set up a crime watch patrol is a healthy use of the energy inside us that allows us to take control of our environment. It tells us that we're not subject to the whims of others or to fate, that we can do something about the world around us.

True Self-Power says the same thing but it concentrates on the manner in which we're able to take command of our personal lives. It is the strength to control our own behavior and internal responses. It helps us build a positive belief about ourselves that remains constant, giving us the self-esteem required to meet the negative influences and unexpected stumbling blocks that are thrown into our paths.

A Man Who Had Self-Power

Bill recognized the value of Self-Power. He paid close attention to this aspect of his personality, understanding that meeting this need would establish an internal base that could protect him against anything that might diminish his self-esteem. He was wise enough to realize that Self-Power was his real power.

Bill's business was hit hard by the slow economy in the late seventies, and after a tough economic struggle, he lost his business. Although he was concerned and unsure of his future, Bill never doubted that he could conquer what he saw as a temporary setback. He trusted his abilities and let his creativity go to work. In a short time, he was up and running. His new company became a huge success. Bill's Self-Power had not let him down, even with an economy over which he had little control. GEM encourages you to pay close attention to your feelings and to listen to what they're telling you. Developing your need for Self-Power gives you the confidence to respect your feelings and to trust your reactions to people and to situations. Self-Power gives you the control to act on your feelings with intelligence and thoughtfulness rather than on impulse.

A Woman Who Lacked Self-Power

Lynn, thirty-eight, was devoted to her family, her community and her career. She was well liked and, for the most part, enjoyed her day-to-day life. What bothered Lynn was her fear of taking risks. She always backed away from the more challenging jobs and avoided the many political positions she had been offered. She convinced her family and friends that she didn't want the added hassles and pressures. But, in fact, Lynn was dying to experience some of these opportunities and felt terrible every time she turned one down.

As she began to explore her past, Lynn quickly discovered the source of her fear. Money had always been scarce when she was growing up and her mother blamed Lynn's father, whom she described as a daydreamer who didn't stick to a secure job.

Most of her school years were spent working to help provide extra income for her family, and she had little time and energy left over for herself. The old message for Lynn was the necessity to establish a secure and stable base rather than to take any risks. Security was her answer to success.

Although she felt loved and self-assured about her value to her family and herself, her picture of the world didn't allow her to believe she had a right to test her potential and to experience her Self-Power. Coming to grips with her need to develop her self-esteem by believing in her own abilities and trusting her own judgment was a major step for Lynn.

It was time for her to recognize that she was not her father, that she was an independent individual with unique talents. She was anything but a daydreamer, and her commitment to people was another quality that protected her from being irresponsible. Freeing herself from the messages of her childhood and creating a new truth about her world allowed Lynn to venture out.

Her success was not a surprise to anyone. But for Lynn these new feelings of self-satisfaction and self-confidence *were* her success.

Her ability to begin making choices that were based only on her belief in herself opened the door for her to grow both professionally and personally. As she challenged herself, Lynn also challenged a society that had not reinforced her need for Self-Power.

When we take the responsibility to nurture our spirit and love ourselves, our Self-Power is able to expand to embrace the belief that we, as unique individuals, have choices and can create personal change.

There is no law against wasted potential. However, failure to develop your Self-Power limits your self-respect and the respect that others will have for you.

Gender Biases Attached to Self-Power

Power means different things to people. The most common gender bias attached to power is that power is a *masculine* term. This bias leaves women feeling powerless and leaves men with an incomplete and misguided understanding of power. In the outside world, this bias may be a reality experienced by both men and women, yet it is not a reality that applies to Self-Power and it does not address Self-Power's purposes, benefits and effects.

Power in the outside world is different from internal power, and until both women and men understand that they need strong Self-Power to protect themselves against the stress of outside power, they cannot live truly effective lives. This external power has placed both men and women at high physical risk. Mental and emotional pressures brought on by society's definition of power can be so overwhelming that it may be necessary to walk away to survive physical health implications.

Due to the bias surrounding outside power as defined for men, it's not easy for men to walk away without experiencing feelings of failure or frustration. Many men can relate to this dilemma because they have experienced this struggle at some point in their lives, especially during a "midlife crisis."

Similarly, this bias is affecting women as more and more choose high-tension careers. Today, for example, less than fifty percent of all managers and administrators in the U.S. are women. They risk loss of self-esteem and image if it appears that they can't hold up under the stresses brought on by this type of power.

In the workplace, both men and women who don't fit the "image" as defined by society suffer a deep sense of conflict, vacillating between adapting to the image or trying to feel okay about who they are.

Historically, men have not been encultured to believe that Self-Power is internal and important to their self-esteem. Instead, this bias separates them from their need for Self-Power, keeping them less in touch with their feelings and operating more from "out of their heads."

Even though social values are changing and many men may go through extensive sensitivity training, the "Good Old Boy Network" still dictates accepted attitudes and behaviors for men.

Your emotions are lost when your brain doesn't have the advantage of drawing from all the down-deep, "inside" information. A gut reaction is often a natural indicator for evaluating a situation or determining an outcome. It is your built-in radar. That's why you hear so much about "women's intuition." It's not anything unique or special; women are encultured to be more comfortable in these areas and to rely on internal messages as a way of assessing infor-mation. This intuitiveness has proved invaluable in the workplace.

Unfortunately, men's relationships with women are also negatively affected by gender bias. Most men deny that they are attracted to women who can think for themselves and are independent. In a quest to feel powerful, these men often ignore or avoid a relationship that has the potential to be mutually rewarding and exciting. The unconscious choice of a woman who appears needy and dependent seems to confirm the man's power. The results are a lifetime of feeling emotionally unfulfilled and a continuous search for personal satisfaction.

Because of the biases attached to power, men find it more difficult to recognize the source of these feelings of dissatisfaction. Overwork, alcohol, extramarital affairs or other unhealthy outlets provide men with temporary compensation for what is missing in their lives.

The gender bias that sex equates to power also inhibits men from experiencing a more meaningful commitment. This produces yet another myth about man's masculinity. Notches in his belt just don't cut it when he needs to feel cared for, loved and appreciated. However, here again, men are robbed of this great experience when they attach Self-Power to a definition that applies only to the wheeling and dealing in their outside world.

A man's bond to his mother often may be his last experience in a warm and trusting relationship. Men with mothers incapable of experiencing their own Self-Power in a caring and loving way are less able to detect their sons' internal need for Self-Power. This increases the chances of a potential void in a man's love relationships.

In summary, a man's society, his family history, his cultural background and his identity as a whole have created a bias about power. This bias keeps him hooked into a belief about himself that does not allow him to understand his desire and need for Self-Power. Focusing on outside power rather than Self-Power decreases a man's chances of experiencing effective relationships and threatens his intimate connections.

The more potent thrust of negative gender bias surrounding power is its effect on women. For thousands of years, women have suffered greatly from the gender bias that power belongs to men and to the outside world. It has been a reality acted out for generations, so it is difficult to dispute.

Because women start by not recognizing Self-Power as an internal need of both genders, they continue to remain in the dark about how to fulfill this need. Most women even find it difficult to acknowledge their right to Self-Power. The difference for men is that they have the opportunity to experience power, at least in the outside world. Women, on the other hand, lack the experience of power within society as well as within themselves.

Another bias involving women and power is that women are too emotional to handle the tough decisions in life and too hysterical in nature to maintain control in their own lives. They are viewed as the weaker sex, unable to meet the demands and pressures of society. Because this bias was accepted as fact and women had few avenues available to challenge it, their need to be dependent on men for financial security entrapped them. Many women remain in relationships that are demeaning and often dangerous, unable to get emotional support or financial assistance to help them create better lives for themselves, and in many cases, their children.

From early childhood, women are taught through cultural beliefs, gender bias and societal inequities that their well-being lies in the hands of men. Therefore, the emphasis for women is not on self-development, but how to support and develop others as a means of making their lives secure.

Even feeling they have a right to succeed creates for some women feelings of guilt and selfishness. With the help of the Women's Movement women now have more resources for support and advancement. Yet gender bias still haunts them and continues to affect their picture of themselves and their world.

Sexuality and Power

A woman's sexual identity also is hooked into a gender bias that teaches her to suppress her natural desires and needs. Fighting this bias is a difficult personal battle. Often, women feel guilt or shame when they experience the pleasure that can be derived through sex. Because they are told that men's egos must be protected, they tend to believe that men must be the sex initiators, pursuers and aggressors.

These messages often keep women timid and unfulfilled. They have not been encouraged to teach men about women's bodies. Until recently, most women went to male OB/GYN specialists whom they referred to as their "female" doctors. More often than not, these male specialists ignored the complaints and needs of their female patients because of their own gender biases.

For most women, gender identity and self-worth can be fulfilled by means other than sex. Some women, however, believe that sex is a woman's only power. Although they may experience pleasurable physical feelings, they are cheated out of a deeper and more meaningful expression of intimacy.

Most men, must confirm their masculinity through sex. Men's sense of identity appears to depend on sexuality. Psychologists generally agree that during adolescence boys obtain non-sexual gains, such as the feeling of power, from

~ ~

masturbation. The capacity for erection is a sign of masculinity and control for a young boy, and his sense of self-worth and identity become strongly attached to the act. As he gets older, it becomes increasingly difficult for him to achieve Self-Power in ways other than by being in control of some object or person.

Considering the confusion surrounding power attached to sex, both women and men give up a lot when sex becomes a control issue or when they accept gender biases that create misperceptions about their sexual identities.

Midlife Crises and Self-Power

One reason so many men face a midlife crisis is that their sexual prowess diminishes or is perceived to diminish as they age. For many, this is a sign that they are no longer in control, that their power is somehow leaving them.

Because they learn to depend on outside power or power over objects and others, as a way of enhancing themselves, men tend not to depend upon their own inner resources and inner feelings to create personal change. They have established less Self-Power on which to build effective lives.

Another reason men are so susceptible to midlife crisis is that they see their power disappearing at work as they reach their late forties and fifties. Younger men come into power, often as bosses of the older man. Because most men never learned the lesson of Self-Power, they're not able to call on their inner strength to carry them through this troubling transition.

They often look to regain their youth in destructive ways, sometimes by divorce and remarriage to a much younger woman, sometimes by a change to a more aggressive, hostile personality. Others wonder how and why life passed them by. They become vaguely discontent, sometimes clinically depressed.

Kevin is a fifty-five-year-old attorney who made an exceptionally fine living during his entire adult life. He has a reasonably happy marriage, three children and a lovely home in a quiet residential area. Kevin works hard, putting in long hours six days a week.

Most people who know Kevin, call him very successful. But Kevin sees himself as a failure, past his prime. He blames college friends who are not financially well off for their own failures. However, when he compares himself to those who have become very rich, Kevin gets upset.

He confided he was in the middle of an affair that he wished to end, but didn't know how. "I love my wife very much," Kevin says, "and it's stupid of me to get involved with this young kid. But for the first time in years, I feel young and important and sexual. If I feel so good about myself, why do I feel so rotten?"

Like men, women also have midlife crises, but for different reasons. Women who are socialized to build their lives and identities around others find themselves at a loss when children leave home or when their partners die, get a divorce, or engage in extramarital affairs.

The loss of roles that gave their lives meaning leads to feelings of depression, apathy, boredom, or loss of enthusiasm in general. A strong sense of Self-Power and the ability to take control of one's own life in order to make change become critical for women and men at this time. Women at this stage must become self-reliant rather than relying on others. Men must reevaluate issues of priority.

~ ~

Women at Work

Women in the workplace are forced to fight their way through negative gender bias that doesn't acknowledge them as competent, talented and bright individuals worthy of powerful positions. Women often find they have to work harder than men to gain and then justify their positions. Because they're not taken as seriously as men, they receive fewer rewards and benefits.

With the increasing numbers of women entering today's work force, the need to confront and challenge these biases should no longer be ignored. The bias that a woman's place is in the home is outdated and unrealistic. When Self-Power is accepted as the key to developing personal success and professional growth, the task of confronting gender biases attached to power becomes easier.

Once women learn to love themselves in a way that opens the door for them to take charge of their destinies, their Self-Power can begin operating in a positive and purposeful way. Once men learn to love themselves in a way that validates their emotional needs, their Self-Power can be internally experienced. Self-Power will give both women and men the confidence to make choices that create meaningful and effective lives.

Chapter Six

Self-Love/Self-Power Relationship: Characteristics

~ ~

When you learn to operate equally out of Self-Love and Self-Power, you will experience the positive relationship they have to one another.

Consider a relationship between two people. For that relationship to develop into a positive experience, the couple must work together toward a healthy balance between one another. Each person must be sensitive to the needs of the other while validating his or her own needs.

The couple must be willing to recognize each other's uniqueness, and be accepting of each other's weaknesses and strengths; this increases their commitment and establishes a stronger bond between them.

The more information and understanding they acquire about one another, the more adept they become at building a solid foundation. When secure foundations are built, relationships survive and grow in respectful and meaningful ways.

Like all "quality" relationships, your relationship with yourself must also be in balance in order to build your internal foundation. This is best accomplished by being sensitive to and fulfilling your need for Self-Love and Self-Power. Self-Love and Self-Power motivate you to succeed, as you define success for *yourself.* Following someone else's idea for success won't give you the freedom to achieve your unique potential.

The GEM Model in Chapter One shows the six internal needs broken into pairs, which form three sets of relationships. Self-Love/Self-Power is the first relationship you must bring into balance.

You grow up and leave your parents, your friends change or move away, you may lose your partner your children become independent and leave the nest, and other close relationships change unexpectedly, but the Self-Love/Self-Power needs stay with you forever. That relationship is you.

The need to build a relationship with yourself that respects your dignity and validates your internal needs is the only way to empower yourself toward effective living. As an adult, only you can control this relationship. The only stumbling blocks to creating internal balance in your Self-Love/Self-Power relationship are the negative messages, real or misinterpreted, you received in your past. They may have been purposeful at one time but more than likely have outlived their original purposes.

As strange as it may seem, people hang on to negative beliefs or behavior out of habit even though they no longer serve any useful purpose. But you can check yourself for such habits and stumbling blocks.

Record Your Own Biases

Write a list of your own biases and prejudices.

Now make two more lists. On one, list the positive messages and beliefs about yourself; on the other, the negative ones. Keep these lists close by as you learn more about the relationship needs of Self-Love and Self-Power.

You will notice that some of what we are discussing is already on your positive list. Don't let go of it. Nurture it. Build on it! Notice what's on your negative list, then ask yourself, "What purpose does it serve in my life now? Do I still need these things in my life?"

After a while, negative beliefs and behavior become patterns that we continue to act on unconsciously. For example, let's say a child reaches out for love, but for whatever reason, the parent or caretaker is unable to provide the love. The negative message received by the child is that she/he is not worth loving. This child could easily grow into an angry, resentful, or depressed adult.

This same child may grow up unaware of the need to develop Self-Love or Self-Power, operating only out of the love need, loving others as a way of trying to get love. Or the grown child may operate only out of the power need, trying to control others to avoid future rejection. Either way, he or she continues to suffer from unrealistic needs for love and power, neither need having anything to do with Self-Love or Self-Power.

The good news is, you can control this relationship. You can change any negative belief or negative behavior. It's important that you be open to this idea, that you trust yourself, and that you test your inner strength. You also must take responsibility for creating positive change and believe you are entitled to it.

~ ~

People Whose Self-Love/Self-Power Needs Are in Balance

Obviously, before you can balance your behavior, you have to be aware of an imbalance. People who have acknowledged their imbalance and are now internally balanced between Self-Love and Self-Power are easily identified by specific observable characteristics.

- *They are sensitive.*

This sensitivity comes out of Self-Love and is expressed through kindness, consideration, gentleness, empathy and other life-loving qualities.

- *They are thoughtful.*

Thoughtful people respect themselves as well as others. They recognize the needs of others and enjoy giving. They do little things that make others feel cared for.

- *They are caring.*

Caring takes time. These people find the time to nurture themselves. They are aware of their own needs as well as the needs of others.

- *They are self-confident.*

They believe in themselves. They like who they are and what they are. They believe in their own potential.

- *They are independent.*

They accept their unique qualities. They believe they have choices, and they are not afraid to take risks. They are resourceful and accept their reality.

- *They are good decision makers.*

They take charge of their lives. They are responsible and trust their judgment. They are not afraid to make mistakes.

- *They enjoy success.*

They have reasonable expectations of people and life; they enjoy self-development and self-growth. They believe they deserve the rewards in life and are willing to work for them. These wise men and women no longer allow their worlds to be controlled by others.

People out of balance in the Self-Love/Self-Power relationship are rarely aware of this imbalance. Over a period of time, they have adopted beliefs and behaviors that are comfortable and familiar. They may not consciously realize that the beliefs and behaviors are negative and ineffective.

In addition to basic survival needs and the GEM needs, every person has internal needs that operate with or without conscious knowledge. One of these is the need for consistency. Whether or not we know it, we all want our behavior to be consistent with our feelings. But when our behavior is inconsistent with our internal Self-Love need we suffer the consequences: anxiety, stress, obsessive and compulsive behaviors, or other psychological or physical problems. When your need for balance between Self-Love and Self-Power is not met, your self-worth and self-esteem are lowered. You react defensively and close off new experiences. You become less effective in your personal life and probably in your work life as well. This imbalance prevents you from enjoying life.

Can You Have Too Much Self-Love or Self-Power?

How much should we love ourselves? How much power should we use to control our own lives? Is there such a thing as too much?

~ ~

Most of us remember the warning messages we got as children: "You're too big for your own britches," or "Think about others before you run off and do whatever you want." Society frowns on people who appear to love themselves so much that they believe everyone else is inferior. If we carry our Self-Power needs to the extreme, we risk offending society or breaking laws. We must consider the "public good" when we take personal action.

If you happen to agree with what is "good" for the public, you have few problems modifying your behavior because old messages still serve a useful purpose. But when you disagree with what significant others consider proper, you will be in conflict. If your need for Self-Power is so strong that you resent others' opinions and advice, your Self-Love could be so little that you take this advice as an attack on your self-esteem.

It is possible to have too much Self-Love or Self-Power in that you could become self-consumed. You might think you don't need to change, and you might be guilty of rationalizing and making excuses for your inappropriate behavior. But assuming you still listen to some of the more reasonable built-in restrictions, you can handle high levels of Self-Love and Self-Power.

For most of us, too much Self-Love or Self-Power isn't the problem. The major problem usually lies in these internal needs being too low or misdirected.

Flip back to Chapter Four and look at your Self-Love/Self-Power test scores. Did you have perfect balance between the two? Were you operating out of too much Self-Love or too much Self-Power? That's important to know. If you operated more out of one than the other rather than both equally, you probably have developed characteristics that get in the way of your living more effectively.

Let's look at two sets of characteristics, those belonging to people who operate out of too little or misdirected Self-Love and those belonging to people who operate out of too little or misdirected Self-Power.

People Whose Self-Love Is Low or Misdirected

- ***They don't separate love from Self-Love.***

They pour their love into others, hoping they will be loved in return.

- ***They build relationships with others instead of themselves.***

This decreases their opportunity to build other positive aspects of their personalities. If they are not careful, they internally diminish their personal value and allow others to take advantage of them.

- ***They have an unrealistic need for approval.***

This need overrides their ability to set limits on others, especially those they love. They will say "yes" when they need to say "no."

- ***They are afraid of rejection.***

They have difficulty communicating their needs to other people, then become resentful or disappointed when others don't meet those needs.

- ***They are too sensitive.***

They are unable to recognize when the problem doesn't belong to them. They often suffer from frustration, depression, anxiety, other kinds of emotional distress, and physical ailments.

- ***They care about others at the cost of not caring about themselves.***

They don't give others the chance to care enough about them. They can't appreciate themselves. Learning to receive is a valuable quality.

- ***They value others more than themselves.***

This makes them doubt their own special talent and limits their potential.

- ***They put their own needs last.***

Meeting others' needs makes them feel important. Often they don't recognize their own needs.

- ***They respect others more than themselves.***

Other people lose respect for them or feel guilty about them. This distances people from them or makes others angry with them.

- ***They don't believe they are deserving.***

Consequently, they often subject themselves to abusive people.

- ***They are passive.***

They're not initiators and don't know how to enjoy the power of their own creativity.

A Man Who Lacked Self-Love

Matt started working with the GEM model at the age of twenty-eight. At his first counseling session he was nervous, uncomfortable and self-conscious. But with prompting, this quiet young man began to share his painful story.

"My girlfriend is divorced and can't seem to hold a job. She lived with her parents, but it was a bad scene, so I took her and her two-year-old son in. I own a landscaping company, but all I'm really doing is cutting grass. I hate it,"

Matt confided. He shared his desire to design unusual and cost-effective landscapes for both commercial and residential properties. The ideas he described were imaginative and artistic. He seemed to have a talent for this business, but promoting himself was another story.

His determination to change his life proved greater than his fears. So with gentle encouragement from the therapist, he reluctantly began to explore his history. This was the very thing he had been avoiding for as long as he could remember.

His mother had suffered from a severe mental disorder that his family didn't acknowledge or talk about. Matt was confused about his mother's mental state and what it was all about.

He described his father as a hard worker who had provided well for Matt and the rest of his family. He also described him as passive, uncommunicative and detached.

When Matt was eight, he was taken to another state by his mother and a man he had never met. It was three weeks before he was located by his father and the police. His mother was taken away. "They told me she was not feeling well and needed a vacation," Matt explained. His mother was institutionalized for the next several months. Her repeated confinement became ordinary in Matt's life, and the entire family acted as though it was not happening.

Matt spoke briefly about his younger brother: "He has problems and we don't have much of a relationship." Except for distant relatives who occasionally stopped in to help, Matt was the primary caretaker for his father, his brother and himself. His artistic ability developed privately, in his bedroom, where he stayed most of the time. He hated school and withdrew into himself. At age sixteen, he got up the nerve to go out for football and made the team, finally finding an activity that involved him with others. But his pattern of behavior was set. Except for his involvement with the team, he remained separate from his classmates.

By the time he came into therapy, Matt had found a girlfriend who was totally dependent upon him. His financial struggle and his own distress hadn't stopped Matt from taking on the responsibility of his girlfriend and her son.

He was operating out of *needing* love from others and not enough Self-Love. Matt is an example of how subconsciously operating out of one internal need in an unhealthy way can compromise the development of the other internal needs.

Matt's history had set him up to have an unrealistic need for love. His personal life as well as his business life were severely handicapped. At age twenty-eight, he had chosen a relationship that lacked fulfillment but allowed him to do what he was comfortable doing: caretaking. His lack of self-confidence stifled his work. He spent his weekends isolated and drinking to numb his feelings. Matt constantly searched for love and approval at great cost to himself. If he said "no" to others, he felt guilty; and if he said "yes," he was burdened.

Matt took the necessary steps and confronted the old messages, the misinterpretations and the painful truths of his past. He took positive measures to change his life. Today, Matt is a successful, highly respected businessman. He replaced troubled relationships with healthy ones. His journey through the GEM relationship needs proved to be therapeutic and a significant journey in his life. His personal stumbling block, i.e., his early socialization messages, had outlived their original purpose. Matt accomplished what he had set out to do.

People Whose Self-Power Is Low or Misdirected

- *They don't separate power from Self-Power.*

Because they haven't satisfied their need for Self-Power, they remain controlled by the outside world.

- *They try to control others.*

They see control as a way of maintaining their power. This decreases the value of their relationships.

- *They are insensitive.*

You cannot have a need to control others and be sensitive to them at the same time.

- *They feel powerful when they are feared.*

They don't understand the difference between being feared and being respected.

- *They are critical.*

They see others as being weaker than they. This makes them less tolerant.

- *They are egotistical.*

They are self-consumed.

- *They isolate themselves.*

They are unable to interact with others in a loving and caring way.

- *They are angry.*

They place undue burdens on themselves and create an unhappy atmosphere.

- *They are not good delegators.*

Good delegators take the time to know people. You must be a good listener if you want to know people well enough to trust them.

- *They are insecure.*

They deny their insecurities, even to themselves.

~ ~

- *They are aggressive.*

They go beyond being assertive when making their needs known. They are demanding and often abusive.

A Woman Who Had Problems With Self-Power

Rita, forty-eight, had reached her goals, so she couldn't understand why she was now unhappy. A past "fling" with a man at work had prompted her to seek help. "I'm not the type to take a chance like this, especially with someone I work with and see as inferior to me," she said.

Rita held a powerful position with an income to match. She had been married eighteen years and had a son attending school overseas. When Rita called for an appointment, she was true to her profile. Within three minutes she had stated her purpose, her expectations and her availability.

She was on time for her first appointment, chose a chair and got down to business. "I'm unhappy with myself and angry that I can't seem to pull myself together. I was … am opposed to therapy, but if it helps, I'll give it a chance."

Rita said she had never felt close to anyone. "I was a military brat, and although travel was interesting and I loved the different cultures, I never had many friends. Dad was big on education and power, and I have him to thank for my position today. Mom had a little drinking problem, nothing bad, but I didn't see much of her. She was a real socialite."

Even though she was an only child, Rita had not received the type of love that helps a child feel approved of and important. Instead, she mostly felt isolated and unnoticed. She learned at an early age to get attention through achievement. And when her need for love wasn't satisfied, she denied the need.

Instead of becoming the "bad girl," she saw her father's powerful position as the answer and used him as her model. The more she achieved, the more she pushed herself. Her family and society rewarded her with praise and recognition, but they didn't know what it was costing her emotionally.

Like Matt, Rita had been deprived of a loving, sensitive childhood. They both had experienced isolation and rejection. Unlike Matt, however, Rita's defense was to avoid the more loving aspects of her personality. She protected herself from rejection by not allowing anyone to penetrate her exterior, which became cold, distant and unfeeling. Rita believed that she could command respect through outside power. Her intelligence and skills overshadowed her insensitivity to others, and her disregard for others was not too surprising, given her history. Her picture of the world did not include Self-Love and Self-Power. Because she lacked an internal foundation that was sensitive to the need to balance her Self-Love and Self-Power relationship, her power was based on the expectations of others.

Rita was consumed with proving herself. She openly admitted to enjoying people fearing her. She didn't know how to have fun and was unable to appreciate others' unique qualities. Instead, she was impatient with their weaknesses. She didn't understand that what she perceived as weakness was, in fact, "humanness."

By trying to be invulnerable, she had not discovered Self-Love, causing her Self-Power to be replaced by other types of power. She was self-centered, and her world revolved mainly around herself, with little room for anyone else. Like others with misdirected power needs, she denied her internal needs.

Fortunately, Rita's "fling" disrupted her historical picture of herself. She was now sensing a void established long ago. The fling wasn't the problem. It was her need to redefine Self-Love and Self-Power. Her brief affair was merely the catalyst for making her aware of deeper emotions and needs.

Working with the GEM model became a challenge for Rita. Dealing with negative aspects of her behavior was painful, but it was the first step toward positive change and the opportunity to re-address her marriage. Rita's husband joined her in therapy, and they worked to establish a better and more intimate relationship.

Rita's outside power is now based on her internal power, her Self-Power. Creating balance in her Self-Love and Self-Power relationship allowed her to make positive change.

As you work toward an equal relationship between Self-Love and Self-Power, your communication with others is less likely to be misinterpreted.

Like Matt and Rita, we strive in different ways to meet our internal needs. Not all of these ways are healthy. All behavior has purpose, and we must be aware of the consequences of our behavior.

GEM should give you a clearer picture of what you need to explore. You should be able to identify your strengths and weaknesses. The journey is far from over, but you are well on your way. Encourage yourself and give yourself credit for taking the first steps. A self-reflective trip is not always easy, but it's an investment in yourself. GEM is the map that will keep you on the right course.

Believe in it!

Chapter Seven

Self-Love/Self-Power Relationship: Key Action Steps

~ ~

The more determined you are to take charge of your life, the more aware you'll become of how you choose your own destiny. With every life journey you take, you'll experience an array of feelings before reaching your destination. These feelings could include anticipation, excitement, joy, sorrow, curiosity, adventure and even exhaustion.

Your journey through Self-Love and Self-Power using the GEM model as your guide led you to a destination where these feelings exist. This internal journey is never-ending, and it's direction is determined by you.

When you meet your need for Self-Love and Self-Power, you continue to develop, grow and achieve. Your life presents you with numerous opportunities to challenge your feelings and thoughts. Your ability to seize each opportunity to learn and grow increases your understanding of yourself and gives you a chance to become all that you can be.

Throughout the Self-Love/Self-Power relationship, you explored how you unconsciously learn about yourself

~ ~

and others and how this affects your behavior. You also
explored how you absorb vast amounts of information
without questioning its meaning or purpose. You need to
question the indirect or subliminal messages you receive
about yourself. It's critical for you to confront any message
implying that you are incapable of loving yourself. Ask
yourself:

Do I accept these messages? Do I know the difference
between Self-Power and outside power and do I know how
that difference effects my life?

My interviews and counseling sessions confirmed that
it's common for people to be unaware of their own biases
and prejudices, so their thoughts are frequently inconsistent
with their feelings. Inconsistency has a direct affect on
behavior. People who lack insight often erect barriers
between their thoughts and their feelings. Imbalance such as
this discourages personal growth and reduces your ability to
communicate effectively.

Exploring Your Family History

The following self-reflective activity will allow you to
go back in time and become conscious of any biases and
prejudices that are still a part of your belief system, and help
you consider how you play them out in your day-to-day life.

The information you gather during this activity will be
helpful when you move on to the Key Action Steps. This is
a simple but direct way to tie together which messages are
barriers, for you and which Key Action Steps will help you
find a solution for removing these barriers. Don't worry if
you can't answer all of the questions; at this point, my only
goal is to help you become more aware of these barriers and

their meaning in your life.

Think about your family members, or the adults who raised you, their personalities, their attitudes, their ideas and their behavior:

1. Were they warm, cold or indifferent?
2. Did you feel loved, protected, encouraged and respected?
3. Who made you feel important while you were growing up? How did they do this?
4. Who did you most respect in your family and why?
5. Who did you feel was the wise adult in your family, and what made you recognize this about them?
6. Who in your family or who in your formative years really listened to you? If no one, whom did you turn to with your questions, doubts and fears?
7. How did your family make decisions?
8. Were you encouraged to brings friends home?
9. Did you have some private space that was acknowledged as yours?
10. Were you expected to contribute? In what way?
11. Was your behavior ever questioned or challenged?
12. How did your parents or guardians treat one another? Was it respectful and loving? Did you see your friends' parents treat each other differently from your own parents? How?
13. If your parents divorced, how did they handle their divorce? Were you put in the middle of it, or were you free to be comfortable with both your mom and dad?

~ ~

14. If the divorce took place before you were old enough to understand the implications or if one of your parents died, who explained the reasons surrounding the divorce or death and who told you about your other parent? How did they present that person to you?
15. What were the household rules and who made them stick?
16. Were these rules reasonable and open to change according to the circumstances?
17. Was there serious physical illness or serious mental or emotional problems in your family? If so, how was it treated and how did you feel about it?
18. Did you ever experience feelings of guilt about any of your family members? Think hard about this question: Who made you feel guilty and how?
19. If you had brothers or sisters, how did they treat you? How were they like you? How were they different? Did your parents treat them differently than they treated you, and if so, how?
20. Was there a favorite child, and, if so, how did you know that?
21. What was your happiest childhood memory?
22. What was your saddest childhood memory?

Continue on the same sheet of paper and answer the additional questions according to your gender:

Men

1. Who was your role model?
2. Can you accept the weaknesses of that person?

3. What negative bias do you have about women that affects how you interact with them today? This answer may not be obvious. So dig deep for that honest but quiet truth hidden inside of you.

4. Through your behavior, how do you aggressively or subtly act out this bias? By the way, everyone has some negative bias about the opposite sex, so if you cannot answer this question, you are denying its existence.

5. Name one Self-Love characteristic that you would like to develop. Examples: humor, sensitivity, self-respect, taking better care of yourself, etc.

6. Name one Self-Power characteristic that you would like to develop. Examples: ability to make good decisions, self-confidence, enjoyment of personal success, etc.

7. Name one prejudice you adopted into your picture of the world that you now recognize came from your family of origin.

8. What is the Number One message about yourself that you received from your past? Have you ever challenged it?

9. Was there a particular behavior or image that your family expected you to adhere to that was uncomfortable for you?

10. What do you like most about being male? What do you like least?

Women

1. Who was your role model?
2. Can you accept the weaknesses of that person?

~ ~

3. What negative bias do you have about men that affects how you interact with them today? This answer may not be obvious. So dig deep for that honest but quiet truth hidden inside of you.

4. Through your behavior, how do you aggressively or subtly act out this bias? By the way, everyone has some negative bias about the opposite sex, so if you cannot answer this question, you are denying its existence.

5. Name one Self-Love characteristic that you would like to develop. Examples: taking better care of yourself, humor, sensitivity, self-respect, etc.

6. Name one Self-Power characteristic that you would like to develop. Example: feeling more important, self-confidence, becoming more decisive, etc.

7. Name one prejudice you adopted into your picture of the world that you now recognize came from your family of origin.

8. What is the Number One message about yourself that you received from your past? Have you ever challenged it?

9. What negative belief about yourself have you convinced yourself is unchangeable? (Look for the Key Action Steps that will confront this belief or message and make it your first challenge, but don't expect immediate change.)

10. What was the most positive message you received about being female? What was the most negative?

Self-Love/Self-Power Key Action Steps
How to Increase Your Self-Love in Your Personal Life:

- ***Step 1. Take the chip off your shoulder.***

It weighs so much it will drag you down. It makes you unable to function effectively. Skip the complaints and the excuses; they're only roadblocks. Remember, any anger you feel toward others will soon be turned inward. Few of us want to be known as a bitter, hostile person. It's a negative label, and when it's attached to you, it will become impossible to feel good about yourself.

- ***Step 2. Correct your mistaken beliefs.***

False assumptions lead to false conclusions. Unreasonable ideas about ourselves and others place us in a state of endless frustration, guilt, anxiety or apathy. The behavior tied to these feelings is likely to be ineffective, unsuccessful and dysfunctional. It will diminish your feelings of self-worth and self-esteem. A few common, but unreasonable, mistaken beliefs about life include:

Myth 1: Nearly everybody should like us.

Reality: If we spend our lives trying to get everyone to like us, we never have time to do anything else.

Myth 2: If we change our environment, we'll find a magic solution to our problems.

Reality: We carry our troubles with us, so be careful not to run away from the problem. A new location will not let you escape.

Myth 3: Our happiness and emotional health are determined by outside forces.

Reality: We're responsible for our own happiness.

Myth 4: Normal, well-adjusted people are always happy.

Reality: Impossible. No one is happy all of the time.

Myth 5: If someone I like learns about the real me, they'll never like or love me.

Reality: True love or friendship is not possible until one gets to know the real person. It's worth taking the risk of rejection.

- ### *Step 3. Affirm yourself.*

Each morning for one week, look at yourself in the mirror and find something you appreciate about yourself. Tell yourself aloud how much you appreciate this quality or attribute. Repeat these affirmations every day. This step is often difficult to do, but hang in there. Examples: "I appreciate my sense of loyalty," "I appreciate my sense of humor."

- ### *Step 4. Pamper yourself.*

Invest in yourself. Plan a shopping trip in which you only purchase something for yourself. Don't buy anything for anyone else. Be aware of whatever messages you have received about being good to yourself. Many men hate to shop, but give it your best shot!

Think about a new look for yourself, be it a hairstyle or a new way of dressing. Take up a new pastime, hobby or whatever else you thought about but never tried. Try to achieve this. It doesn't have to be something drastic. Set aside a day or evening to pamper yourself. You need to know how to feel special.

Ask for others' cooperation by letting them know that you will be doing this. Expect their support, but if you don't get it, do it anyway.

- ### *Step 5. Get control of your body and your health.*

If you need to increase your level of Self-Love, one of the best places to start is with your own body and health.

Once you get control of this, it will be much easier for you to gain control of other areas that increase your Self-Love.

Start with a good, sensible, diet as free from fat as possible. Exercise at least a few minutes every day by doing anything you enjoy. The energy you develop from good eating and exercise habits will give you the strength to increase your overall Self-Love.

- ***Step 6. Learn to forgive yourself.***

Forgiveness is the key to Self-Love. As long as you are hard on yourself, you give others the permission to be hard on you, too. We all have said things, felt things and done things we're not proud of. So what! Forgive yourself and get on with positive actions. Self-punishment is a waste of energy.

- ***Step 7. Laugh at your mistakes ... then learn from them.***

Find the humor in errors. Recognize that your mistakes are your learning opportunities. Remember, there is no such thing as failure. There are only successes that you don't like!

- ***Step 8. Talk to Yourself.***

Each time a negative thought or feeling surfaces, remind yourself that you choose what you think and feel. Replace the negative with a positive. Keep in mind that when you say I can't, what you really mean is I won't. It's your choice!

- ***Step 9. Set personal goals.***

List five positive goals you would like to achieve within the next three months. Pick goals that you are not currently allowing yourself to accomplish. These unaccomplished goals have been confirming your feelings of inadequacy. Make sure these goals are reasonable. Make sure that they are not attached to someone else and that they're within your total control. Don't set yourself up to be unsuccessful.

~ ~

- *Step 10. Learn to be good at receiving.*

Ask someone to give you something. It can be anything of your choosing, just so it's reasonable and within that person's capacity to give. Too often we ask for something, knowing another is unable to give it.

- *Step 11. Accept that you are worth loving.*

Your final step for building self-worth is to meet your need for Self-Love. Believe that you are a loving and lovable person. Create a new picture of yourself that is loving. Understand that you first must love yourself — and why not? Don't let anything or anyone paint a different picture for you.

Others will see only the picture you paint, so make it beautiful through warm, forgiving and loving actions to yourself. It's your life, and you have the right to make it all that you can. You deserve it. Nurturing yourself feels wonderful and sends you on your way to internal balance.

How to Increase Your Self-Love in Your Work Life:

- *Step 1. Don't get stuck by your drive for perfection.*

Some of us are so worried about doing everything perfectly that we never get out of first gear. In business, there's no such thing as a successful person who is perfect at everything she or he does. There are too many decisions to be made during the day, too many problems to solve and too many opportunities to create change. When you wait for perfection, nothing happens.

Successful, effective people do the best they can with the information they have. Their decisions don't have to be 100% perfect. Empower yourself by letting go of your need for perfection.

- ***Step 2. Don't put everyone else on a pedestal.***

It's smart to admire successful people, to use them as role models and mentors. But success doesn't mean they're any better or smarter than you. Like everyone else in this world, they have their weaknesses and problems.

It's time for you to believe an absolute fact: You're not the only one who makes mistakes, nor are you the only one who wonders if you made the right decision. Successful people accept their mistakes along with their good decisions.

Unless they inherited their wealth, they, too, started from the bottom. They moved slowly in the beginning, but forced themselves to test the waters. They made decisions they were unsure about and learned to live with the consequences. They took what came with the territory, including their own lack of certainty. When they were wrong, they learned from their mistakes; when they were right, they enjoyed it. Did you know that a survey of the country's top chief executive officers revealed that their average grade at graduation from college was only a "C"? You need to like yourself even when you make a colossal mistake. Take pride in your determination to learn from your mistakes, and you, too, will start to become more effective at work.

- ***Step 3. Choose your career carefully.***

Don't rush into a career just because you heard that it offers a good income. Working at a job or a career that you don't enjoy can stifle your creativity and diminish your enthusiasm. On the other hand, when chosen properly, a career can trigger you to focus on your potential.

So take extra time to find the career that suits your personality. Ask yourself what you'd really like to do if you had unlimited money. Then, if possible, find a way to do

~ ~

that and get paid for it. Testing is available at a reasonable cost; it can help you make a good match between your personality and your career. Take advantage of it. You'll like yourself much more when you're in a job that fulfills your internal needs.

- ***Step 4. Learn to say no.***

If you don't learn to say no, you'll never meet deadlines, and you'll fail to operate effectively at work. You need to take control of your time and take control of what you do with that time. I don't mean you should say no when you're asked to do something that is part of your job. Nor am I suggesting that you become negative when people seek help from you. But you must learn to evaluate requests made of you. Meeting your need for Self-Love helps you to say no without feeling guilty or fearful. And it helps you to say yes to what is important!

- ***Step 5. Learn to ask questions.***

Asking well thought out questions is a good way to learn. People who feel good about themselves don't have a need to know it all. They recognize that a real expert is someone who is secure enough to go to an expert.

Remember, successful people like to help, so take advantage of this opportunity to learn.

- ***Step 6. Become sensitive to others.***

Take the time to recognize that everyone has a need for approval and acceptance. See them, regardless of their behavior, as people who are trying to get their needs met in the best way they know how. Don't be harsh in your judgment of them. For your own sake, especially for your own growth, be willing to see beyond the surface. If their behavior is intolerable, look for a solution that is constructive and not self-serving.

- ***Step 7. Acquire a thicker skin.***

Overly sensitive people overreact. This leads to ineffective communication and defensiveness. People with low Self-Love are thin-skinned.

If you find yourself being defensive, ask yourself what is making you feel insecure. Be willing to see how you participate in ineffective communication and take responsibility for this participation.

- ***Step 8. Pattern yourself after people you admire.***

If low Self-Love is your problem, look for men and women whom you respect and admire. Notice their attitudes and behavior. Ask them how they feel about their jobs and their place in life. Listen to what they say and how they say it. Don't be timid — most people enjoy talking about themselves if the information being asked isn't too personal. Incorporate anything you learn from these folks that suits your own personality. Then start behaving according to these new standards. At first, it may feel awkward, but it's worth trying. If you're successful, you'll start liking yourself better because you will be following a self-approved behavior path—one that you selected and adapted to suit your own personality.

- ***Step 9. Take risks.***

It's always a risk to challenge the unknown. But taking a risk will teach you more about yourself. It's often the only way to uncover your hidden talents or experience your personal areas of strength. Ask yourself, "What is the worst thing that could happen to me if I take this risk?" If you can live with the answer, do it! You have nothing to lose and everything to gain. These are the "good" risks. Building our Self-Love requires testing ourselves.

~ ~

How to Increase Your Self-Power in Your Personal Life:

- *Step 1. Deal with the present; experience the here and now.*

Successful people concentrate on changing what can be changed—the present. Direct your Self-Power to targets that are guaranteed to respond: your present actions, your present thoughts, your present beliefs. Live in the present and concentrate on changing what needs to be changed now!

- *Step 2. Set yourself up for success.*

The best way to increase your self-esteem is to accomplish goals. Self-Power goals are always reasonable and attainable, yet they test your potential and stretch you beyond your comfort zone. When you make your goals reasonable, you set yourself up for success. Goals that are too hard to reach produce failure.

Start off by setting simple goals. When you achieve them, you'll feel good about yourself. That good feeling is your positive reward and reinforces your self-esteem. This will help build your self-confidence slowly and properly and will enable you to handle more difficult goals as you go along.

- *Step 3. Modify your behavior with positive reinforcement.*

You can release your potential energy by learning new, effective behavior and letting go of ineffective behavior. If you want to take control of your own destiny, reward yourself with each successful step you take.

An effective behavior modification might be to try making some simple, quick change. When you accomplish this change, reinforce the new behavior immediately. Give yourself a reward: a nice dinner, a new suit or dress, maybe a piece of art. It may be something less extravagant like a movie or a book. Whatever. It's your accomplishment, therefore, it's your reward. Any self-nurturing reminder feels good and connects the good feelings with the new behavior.

- ***Step 4. Learn to be clear about your limits.***

Respecting yourself and commanding respect from others is necessary if you intend to strengthen your self-esteem. This can't be done unless you know how to set limits on yourself and others. Setting a limit or drawing an imaginary boundary line allows others, as well as yourself, to know some of the following information about you:

- Where you stand on an issue.
- How much or how little you intend to be involved.
- What someone can and can't expect from you.
- What you expect from others.
- At what point you feel someone is stepping over the line with you and what type of signals they can expect from you in order to know that.

- ***Step 5. Adopt new interests.***

Self-confidence leads to Self-Power. One of the best ways to develop self-confidence is to acquire a variety of new interests without pushing yourself to excel in all of them. Doing something new without being concerned about whether you do it well produces a feeling of freedom.

If you make up your mind to try the new activity just for fun, you remove the pressure to succeed. By doing something new and different, you'll break away from old behavior, become liberated, and experience new truths about your capabilities.

~ ~

- ***Step 6. Become familiar with social reality.***

It's not only important to know yourself; you also must understand what others expect of you. You need to recognize the realities of the outside world. When you learn how society works, you're better able to make positive behavior changes. You become successful at blending with others rather than acting defensively or blaming others for your ineffectiveness.

One of the best ways you can become of value to others is by knowing what they want from you. As you learn about others you learn more about the outside world. When you alter your actions to become more constructive, you'll gain self-respect and command respect from others.

- ***Step 7. Learn to trust your own judgment.***

Making a mistake once in a while doesn't mean your judgment is poor. Empower yourself by building trust in your own judgments and acting on them.

Start with less important decisions and slowly experience the feeling of trusting your own judgment and standing behind it. Each time you do this, you will build your self-confidence and self-esteem.

Good decision makers accept that their decisions won't always be right. But they trust their judgment enough to know that they can recover from decisions that don't work out.

- ***Step 8. Do the unexpected.***

Pull yourself out of any ruts you've gotten into. Let yourself feel discomfort just long enough to try something new and different. Better to be a little uncomfortable than bored. Examine your old behavior and think about an alternative behavior. Try it. You can always go back to the old if the new isn't working.

- ***Step 9. Let your actions speak louder than your words.***

Your personal life will have more meaning when your actions match your words. Too often, people speak the right words but their actions are contradictory. Eventually they're not taken seriously by others. They lose their effectiveness, and their Self-Power decreases. So think before you make important statements, and know that you can support your statements through your actions.

How to Increase Your Self-Power in Your Work Life:

- ***Step 1. Work to improve your skills.***

Most of us want to get ahead at work, to get promoted, to earn more money. Once in a blue moon, a promotion is offered without our doing anything special to earn it. But how many times have you seen a blue moon? Not many!

You already have the basic ingredients you need to get ahead — your own potential.

Learn to use your potential to create the positive change that you want in your career. You need a competitive edge. You can get that competitive edge several ways:

- Ask yourself if more training or an advanced education would help make you a better candidate for promotion. If you're not sure about this, ask your boss or someone else you respect. If the answer is "yes," you can improve your level of education by taking courses at a local community college or university. Your employer may pay a portion of the tuition; no harm in asserting yourself by asking.

~ ~

- Find a mentor in your company. Mentors are important to you because they can help energize your Self-Power and make it work more effectively. Make a list of the most respected, most powerful, most upwardly mobile women and men in the firm and introduce yourself to them. Develop a rapport by getting to know them.

  Ask their advice about something they excel in, letting them know about your desire to learn. Then ask if they'll show you the ropes or if you can use them as a sounding board for your ideas.

- Learn to get along with others. People skills are important at work. When you know how to work well with others, to make them feel good about themselves, their enthusiasm and excitement will add to yours. Your power to make constructive change will be charged by the positive energy you receive from co-workers and peers who enjoy working with you.

- Show genuine interest in other people. Practice listening, not always talking. Help someone feel good about herself or himself. Make only sincere and accurate statements. You'll be amazed at people's positive reactions. You'll leave the room revved up and ready to take on the world.

- *Step 2. Learn to control your time.*

  People who would rather blame others or cast their fate to the winds often cite lack of time as a reason for not making improvements in their lives. We all start with

~ ~

the same amount of available time, so time isn't the problem.

It's what we do with our time that makes the difference. Some people have a good sense of time and make it work for them. You can, too. The first step is to accept that you will have to spend time on things that aren't pleasing to you. Do these things first then move on to what you like to do. Pace yourself. Timing is everything!

- ***Step 3. Learn to prioritize your goals.***

Know which goals are important to you and spend your time on them. Drop the wasted effort and energy it takes to achieve unimportant goals. The definition between important and unimportant is up to you. You can separate the important goals from the less important goals by listing all of your goals on a piece of paper and prioritizing them.

Some helpful hints about successful goal setting:
- Goals should be your own; they should serve your needs.
- They should be written down.
- They should be realistic, obtainable, specific and measurable.
- They should have a timetable.
- They should be compatible with one another. Remember, they need to be within your total control.

- ***Step 4. Learn to be responsible only for yourself.***

Too often, we take on the responsibility for others when it's not our role. Other than a responsibility to someone that you supervise or manage, your first responsibility must be to yourself. Don't waste valuable time and energy trying to think or feel for another person. Be responsible for your own actions, your own tasks and your own professional growth.

~ ~

- ### Step 5. Is the glass half full or half empty?

Don't kid yourself. A negative attitude can make or break your potential success. How you choose to sum up a situation or a person can make a big difference in your attitude. Studies have shown that positive, upbeat people generally experience more success then negative people. A positive attitude can keep your adrenaline running in the face of disappointment and give you the positive energy to conquer a problem.

- ### Step 6. Learn to delegate.

You can't be as effective as you need to be at work if you do everything yourself. If you're a manager or a supervisor, get those who work for you to do some of your more routine work. Give them the opportunity to learn while at the same time freeing you to be more innovative and creative in running your department.

If you are not a manager, you can still delegate work. You can get others to do job functions that don't require your specific skills. Secretaries, for example, can get travel agents to check airline schedules; maintenance personnel to fix equipment; the typing or word-processing pool to turn out long, detailed reports; and clerks to file papers. Trusting others to do this work leaves you more time for important planning or for other functions that will give you visibility or will be meaningful to you. Once you stop counting only on yourself and look to others, their accomplishments will add to yours. Your Self-Power, which enables you to become effective and successful, will double or triple.

- ### Step 7. Stick for a long time with what you need to get done.

If you want to get ahead at work, don't give up on tough assignments. Stick to it as long as you are making progress. Your actions affect people who may resist your efforts because they don't want to change. But if the goal is important — empowering yourself at work certainly is — don't lose patience. By quitting too soon, you may be giving up just minutes before success.

- ***Step 8. Work intently.***

Making changes to your work environment and your place in it is never easy. It takes hard work. Even when you're not specifically trying to change anything, hard work may help make you visible, and you may be rewarded with raises and promotions. Even if it's not recognized, a side benefit of hard work is the good feeling you get when you achieve your goal. When you work hard, you know the accomplishment was due to your effort rather than luck or some outside force.

- ***Step 9. Take advantage of luck.***

When you are the beneficiary of a stroke of luck, take advantage of it. Build on it with your own actions rather than waiting for another bolt of lightning luck to strike in the same place. Personal effort doubles or triples the benefits of luck. By the way, you may not believe it now, but you're probably a wonderful person and deserve all the good luck that comes your way. So enjoy it, and let it help you operate more effectively.

- ***Step 10. Accept your success without feeling guilty.***

Women who were brought up to believe that their role is to stay at home to care for their families sometimes feel guilty when they're successful at work. It's understandable that we might experience some pangs of guilt when performing a non-traditional role.

Both men and women can feel guilty about their success in the work world. Promotions and high income often come at the expense of spending time with one's family. If you and your family agree that the income and security you've achieved is important to all of you as a unit, be pleased that you've accomplished this family goal. If other family members want your presence, rather than the income, re-examine your priorities. Good relationships acknowledge the value of accommodation. However, never forget that your uniqueness enhances a relationship, so don't lose who you are when you prioritize. You still need to feel that your own needs are being met, that they are important and worth your attention and respect.

Making the Choice

Self-Love and Self-Power will always be the two most important needs for you to meet. By choosing to create a balance between these two needs, you are electing to communicate and conduct your life in a reasonable, happy and effective way.

Before we move on to the next GEM relationship— Intimacy/Solitude, take some time to relax and reflect on exactly what Self-Love and Self-Power mean to you. Understand that developing the ability to meet these needs is your responsibility and within your total control. It is your choice.

Chapter Eight

Intimacy/Solitude Relationship: Issues

~ ~

Do you communicate your thoughts easily? Do you feel happy and content when you're alone? Are the internal feelings you most experience more positive than negative? Are the relationships in your life meaningful and easy to enjoy, or do they disappoint you and often leave you feeling unsatisfied? Your journey into the second pair of GEM needs, Intimacy and Solitude, will help you answer these questions.

Intimacy and Solitude are delicate internal needs that lie deep within you. Within our families and our societies, most women and men were socialized in ways that discouraged open communication and deep levels of understanding.

This narrow-minded socialization process discourages people from paying close attention to their needs for Intimacy and Solitude. Because of this, they deny themselves the enthusiastic and passionate personality characteristics that evolve from satisfying these special needs.

~ ~

Intimacy and Solitude influence attitudes and behavior. Are you "self" aware of your thoughts and actions, especially when satisfying these two needs?

Awareness will reduce any fear you have about self-disclosure and self-evaluation. Respect for yourself and others as well as respect from others cannot thrive on limited insight and restricted communication.

Disturbing feelings are a major obstacle when seeking Intimacy and Solitude. Most people will try to ignore unpleasant feelings. But these types of feelings can tell us a great deal about ourselves. If you endure some of the distress accompanying these feelings, your awareness will increase, and you will tap into new information about yourself. This chapter examines such sensitive personal issues as trust, vulnerability, introspection, love and friend-ship. We hope you will stretch yourself by probing deep into your feelings.

Let's re-examine our definitions of Intimacy and Solitude:

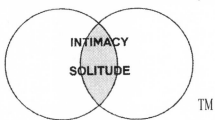

Intimacy: the capability for honest self-disclosure; it is the ability to trust yourself and others in order to experience close and deep levels of communication; an absence of fear that allows you the freedom to be vulnerable.

Solitude: the inner strength to stand alone when necessary; it is a sense of independence and internal self-control that implies competence to deal with life.

~ ~

As you journey into this second GEM relationship, try to remain conscious of these definitions. They are a reminder of the rewards of increasing your capacity for Intimacy and learning to enjoy your Solitude, rather than fearing it.

The Intimacy Need

Have you ever felt out of sorts, with your enthusiasm at a low point, feeling empty and uninvolved? During such a time, you probably felt you were not getting enough comfort and inner peace. Or, maybe you can remember walking away from a conversation feeling as though you hadn't said what you really wanted to say; you felt misunderstood and unappreciated.

When such feelings occur, they aren't necessarily all that important, but when these feelings linger or surface on a regular basis, they become uncomfortable. This discomfort may be sending you a warning. Your built-in radar may be alerting you to internal conflict.

Each of us has a wonderful internal mechanism that triggers an inner reaction or feeling whenever we are in conflict. This mechanism is often referred to as a gut feeling or intuition. Most people do not recognize or appreciate this personal mechanism, so they don't use this built-in radar to its best advantage.

Ignoring the warning signal can cost you the opportunity for continued personal growth and development, and valuable insights.

Becoming more in tune with yourself is a way to begin relying on this internal system. It also helps you to trust your personal protector, your internal voice. With the help of this internal reaction system, you are better

~ ~

equipped to understand the lessons involved in all situations, circumstances and relationships. Your built-in radar can be your best advisor or counselor. It acts only on your behalf. But you must know how to listen for it, you must trust it, and you must have the self-confidence to act upon it.

This can only happen when you believe in the process of becoming Intimate with yourself — a process that is alien to many people.

The Intimate Self

You can't expect to understand and know others or expect others to understand and know you if you remain distant from your innermost self. Distance from this self keeps you distant from your feelings. When you're distant from your feelings, your built-in radar can't work for you in a healthy way.

Out of fear, many people avoid the deep level of self-honesty or self-disclosure that unlocks the door to the Intimate Self. But neither your personal nor your work relationships can be effective unless your communication style encompasses honesty, caring, openness and respect.

A deep level of self-awareness and self-honesty is the basis for your deeper truths — truths, that if faced, help you to be more forgiving of and loving to yourself. In certain situations and in special relationships, you need to be secure enough to risk being vulnerable. If you have enough self-confidence to know when to exercise your vulnerability, you will experience the joys of intimacy. Vulnerability doesn't have to mean a loss of control of yourself or a loss of control in your life.

Fear of Being Vulnerable

Jill was thirty-seven when she sought counseling. She was unhappy about the relationships in her life. She described them as being superficial and guarded. As she turned inward to her Intimate Self, she began to find her deeper truths and discover the reasons for her shyness.

Her aloofness was only a defense against her agonizing fear of abandonment and rejection. Based on her past, her fear was not unfounded, but it was critical for her to overcome this fear to achieve the happiness she was looking for. Jill needed to understand how messages from her past were affecting her present behavior. She needed to realize how her fear of being vulnerable was interfering with her need to have close and loving relationships. Orphaned at five months, Jill lived in an orphanage until she was seventeen, at which time she was adopted by an older couple. Along with the love she so desperately needed, they also provided her with an excellent education and a sense of security. Unfortunately, her adoptive parents died within a year of one another, leaving Jill alone at age twenty-seven. Ten years of a loving family had not been enough time for Jill to heal emotionally and fill the emptiness of her deprived childhood.

She was overwhelmed by the loss of the only family she had ever known, and when she entered therapy she had not yet grieved her adoptive parents' deaths. She perceived this loss as complete abandonment and rejection. Jill needed a loving support system, and more time to overcome her feelings of emptiness. She still doubted her worth and questioned whether she deserved to be loved. She felt powerless and lonely.

~ ~

The questions surrounding her vulnerability and her low Self-Power were painful to address. Until therapy, she hadn't felt comfortable or confident enough to journey deep into her Intimate Self. She had remained cautious, operating only out of the old messages of her past. To Jill, these messages were clear as she repeated over and over again, "I'm not meant to be happy, I'm not meant to be happy."

Jill slowly peeled away her protective layers to explore deep within herself. The old pain, her grief and suffering started to surface. As difficult as this was, Jill allowed herself to become vulnerable enough to confront what had created her loneliness.

Jill commented on several occasions, "I can't believe that letting myself feel something as painful as this can, at the same time, make me feel so good." Jill was describing the relief that comes when pain is no longer repressed and hurtful feelings surface for the purpose of emotional healing. She had discovered the emotional strength of choosing to heal.

We experience Self-Power when we learn the difference between making a choice to be vulnerable for positive reasons and making no choice because we feel helpless.

As Jill's therapy continued, she experienced the value of exploring that hidden place inside (what some therapists might refer to as her "Inner Child") as a step toward building an effective life — a life that could allow Jill to establish loving relationships. With the help and support of counseling, Jill began to appreciate her Intimate Self. This appreciation helped her to accept the important insights that her vulnerability and her pain provided.

Jill needed to experience these insights in order to reach a positive level of Intimacy. Until she got close to herself, this lovely woman's relationships could only be greatly compromised. Accepting this need and interpreting it positively empowered her and helped her develop the relationship skills that Intimacy with self and others provides.

Trusting

The ability to trust yourself and others is a major aspect of Intimacy. Trust begins in the earliest years of life. During infancy, you are totally dependent on another for your every need. Not having one's needs met during this period in a way that is adequate, consistent and comforting can diminish your ability to trust. When your ability to trust is limited, your picture of yourself and others becomes shaded in negative ways; your actions and reactions tend to be more negative than positive.

When your sense of self is centered and stabilized, you can trust yourself more. This builds self-confidence and frees you to seek whatever options and alternatives are available to you. People who trust themselves are more relaxed than those who remain guarded and suspicious. Trusting encourages honesty, and honesty encourages good communication.

A Man Who Didn't Trust

David's distrust of people continually got in the way of a more relaxed life. In his attempt to lessen his anxiety, he spent most of his time and energy mentally reliving and rethinking day-to-day situations and conversations. His suspicious nature was easy to understand when he told his story.

"While growing up, I was led to believe that my family didn't have much money. My Dad owned and operated a small store that appeared to be successful. Yet, I was continually reminded by my mother that times were tough and that both she and my father had to make great sacrifices for my sister and me.

"My sister only worked in Dad's store occasionally. I worked there every day from the time I was nine years old until I was thirteen.

"At first, I thought of it as fun, until I got my first real job outside of the family business. I was expected to contribute whatever I made to the household, and the household, I came to learn, was my mother."

David's mother was demanding and demeaning. More important, David found he couldn't trust her. "I heard her lie to customers, to family members, even to my father. She didn't seem to know how to tell the truth. No one seemed to notice this or question her. Once I asked my father about her lying, and he told me to ignore it. He also made it plain that this was a subject he didn't intend to discuss."

When his father died, David uncovered the true wealth of his parents. It was considerable. His early fears about the family's finances and his embarrassment about not having the same things as his boyhood friends had been unnecessary. He felt great resentment when he remembered how he had struggled to put himself through college. He said he felt betrayed, humiliated and fooled by his own parents.

As David journeyed back through his past, he recalled more times when he felt humiliated for believing in a person or in a situation that turned out to be different from the way it was originally presented. By his early teens, David had cut off the good feelings that come from establishing trusting relationships. Instead, his life was filled with noncommittal relationships and constant feelings of pending doom and anxiety. David was a classic example of the children's story, "Chicken Little," in which the fatalist fowl constantly laments, "The sky is falling, the sky is falling!"

The energy David spent keeping his anxiety under control finally caught up with his physical health. He entered into counseling after much insistence by his medical doctor.

At first, David could not see any connection between his physical symptoms and his psychological outlook. To him, his past was his past, and the process of probing into his Intimate Self and his early history seemed irrelevant.

But once he learned that the process he used for solving business problems was similar to the process he needed to gain personal insight (collecting information and investigation), it became easier for him to grasp the connection. He came to see his behavior more clearly and to understand how his anxiety attacks were linked to his suspiciousness and feelings of distrust.

Feelings of Intimacy were foreign to David. His need to remain cut off and distant in order to feel safe and free of disappointment held him back from satisfying his Intimacy need. His lack of trust prevented him from getting close to himself or anyone else, and he realized he had never had a positive experience with Intimacy.

With great effort, David began creating change in his life. He grew to trust himself more, and this gave him more emotional comfort. He shared the fact that his life had changed on many levels.

"My company has never run so well. My time is better allocated, my wife and I talk more and in general, I feel less anxious and more in control. I will probably continue to have the need to double-check everything, however, but at least I can trust myself enough to recognize when to let it

~ ~

go." It took a lot of work, but the outcome was well worth David's effort. He is a perfect example of how important Intimacy is in achieving a positive personal and professional life.

Family History

Starting early in life, we build protective layers around our thoughts and feelings to shield us from emotional pain. Painful feelings are usually a result of ridicule, rejection, disapproval, deprivation, abuse or other emotional hurts inflicted on us by others.

Learning to protect yourself from emotional pain is not all bad. In certain circumstances, it is wise to find healthy ways to minimize pain. In fact, the ability to minimize emotional pain can help you survive many things and can strengthen your effectiveness.

If you have learned to protect yourself, you may be better able to roll with the punches, so to speak; you are more flexible and can operate in ways that help you move beyond something negative. But if you disguise or numb your feelings to the degree that you do not acknowledge their existence (much like David did), your perceptions become unclear and often inaccurate. Protecting yourself to this degree causes you to move away from your true feelings. This keeps you out of touch with your wants and needs. In this way, you continue ignoring your need for Intimacy. Peeling away these layers of protective insulation will lead you to your Intimate Self.

You have probably read or heard, "The truth shall set you free." This statement makes good sense. Take a moment to try to understand how this statement might apply to you. Think about a time when you avoided the truth in your

~ ~

effort to avoid emotional pain. Now ask yourself the following questions:

1. How long was I able to avoid the pain? A day? A week? A year?
2. At some point in time, did I not have to face the situation, issue or dilemma?
3. Did I experience a sense of relief when I faced whatever it was I had to face, in spite of the pain attached to it?
4. Was this not the exact point in time when I could finally look for the answer or the solution?

Becoming intimate with yourself increases your ability to solve problems because it increases your insight and objectivity. Honesty combined with self-awareness enhances problem-solving skills.

Intimacy and Others

Unfortunately, many people believe that the expression of Intimacy is limited to their private lives or is exclusive only to a love relationship or to sex. They do not understand the importance or the extent of the role that Intimacy plays in their interactions with the people they work or socialize with.

Intimacy has different levels and can be expressed in different ways. All levels of Intimacy have an appropriate place and all levels are valuable. Many people limit their experience of Intimacy only because they do not understand it.

But the good communicators, the effective rapport builders and some of the most sincere and successful people acknowledge and meet their need for Intimacy. They put the fear of being vulnerable behind them. They are comfortable

~ ~

in their belief that Intimacy is one of the main paths to a deep level of friendship with themselves and with significant people in their lives. They recognize that sex is only a physical expression of Intimacy.

Intimacy offers the deepest level of closeness. It is a feeling of self-fulfillment and contentment within yourself and within the relationships you choose. In general, Intimacy occurs whenever someone is supportive of a person in a meaningful way and communicates this support. But remember, the level of your Intimacy with another is determined by the level of your Intimacy with yourself.

Intimacy and Your Health

Your need for Intimacy is crucial to your physical and emotional well-being. Everyone needs to feel connected to someone or something, and this is not accomplished through isolation. It requires communicating, touching, listening and involvement.

When people fear Intimacy to the extent that they withdraw from closeness, illnesses such as colitis, migraine headaches, ulcers or other stress-related physical symptoms can appear. Individuals may develop emotional illnesses such as obsessive or compulsive behavior, depression, anxiety or other debilitating emotional disorders or physical diseases.

Studies indicate that women and men need to have Intimacy in their lives in order to maintain good health. Your physical and emotional systems are nurtured when this need is met.

Biases and Prejudices Attached to Intimacy

Throughout the chapter on Self-Love and Self-Power, I encouraged you to examine how your past affects your present. Looking at the reasons Jill feared being vulnerable and learning how David lost his willingness to trust were two examples of how a negative experience in the past can be a stumbling block in meeting your need for Intimacy in the present.

Take the time to understand your own definition of Intimacy. You need to reacquaint yourself with how you observed Intimacy between your family members or those with whom you lived. Ask yourself, "What was my experience with Intimacy while I was growing up?" Think back to the messages you received in your childhood about what was good and what was bad about Intimacy. These messages became the basis from which you interpreted the meaning of Intimacy. So it's important to journey back in time as a way to readdress your particular beliefs and feelings. In doing this, you may become aware that you have personal issues or experiences that cause you discomfort and create stress whenever the Intimacy need surfaces.

The following short activity will help you identify some of the old messages you received about Intimacy. Really challenge yourself — this activity can be insightful. Write down any thoughts or feelings that surface. Hang on to these notes, as they will be helpful to you later.

You may not remember ever hearing the word Intimacy, but you may remember certain actions or discussions that today would be labeled as Intimacy. Whether they called it Intimacy or whether they called it something else isn't important. Consider how you were taught to think about openness, sharing, closeness, trust, friendship,

~ ~

vulnerability and honesty. At this moment, notice your feelings. You may feel uncomfortable trying to resurrect old memories, especially if your family didn't have much Intimacy. Perhaps there was so little Intimacy that you feel unsure about what you should be familiar with.

Try to get a clearer vision of these memories and concentrate on the feelings they generate. If you lack these memories or feelings, Intimacy probably was not expressed in your household. You may find you are not meeting this need in your life today and you may be uncomfortable in Intimate situations. Take whatever time you need now to write down your thoughts and feelings.

Gender Biases Attached to Intimacy

The "macho" image, still part of our western society, doesn't include Intimacy as a suitable or valuable characteristic. This bias contends that Intimacy is a sign of weakness. Even males less caught up in society's image have been reared to portray themselves in ways that make them seem brave and in charge. Their manner can appear aloof, unfeeling, tough, or unemotional.

Our society rewards such "less-sensitive" behavior with attention and admiration. Just think about positions of power within our society and government or about the sports heroes we most idolize or admire. Do you think of these people as sensitive and Intimate, or do you recognize that you know little about the Intimate and sensitive sides of their personalities? More times than not, they have been described as tough, hard-hitting individuals, capable of "winning at all costs."

What is that message telling us? It's certainly not suggesting that they are warm, sensitive, Intimate people who "win" due to a sensitive and warm approach to life and people. Quite the opposite!

Another myth about Intimacy, often lived out by men, is that Intimacy is only a sexual expression. This belief robs a person of the opportunity and the experience to communicate effectively.

Intimacy is a means of communicating that draws people closer and establishes the trust necessary for developing trustworthy friendship.

Whenever a bias suggests that a feeling of closeness is an emotion to be guarded against, the underlying message or belief is that vulnerability is an enemy. Look at the notes you took during the last activity. What were some of your beliefs about Intimacy? What feelings and thoughts did you experience during this activity? Remember, the answers lie in your history. Don't be afraid to confront your beliefs because no matter how hard you try to disguise them, your biases and prejudices are played out through your behavior. Be willing to look for them.

Gender bias surrounding Intimacy, including the "macho" image, significantly affects women. Although many women would hate to admit it, they often buy into this bias. They reinforce the bias when they continue to view "macho" behavior as a sign of strength, control or success. This belief can lead them into relationships that lack depth and compassion. After a period of time, these women often find that they are not in a relationship with someone who is strong or in control of her or his life. Instead, they find they are with someone who is likely to be out of control, selfish, narcissistic or even injurious.

This "macho" bias also confuses women about the definition of strength and leads them to question their own ability to succeed. One subtle message suggests that only

~ ~

the most feminine women (whatever that is) can experience Intimacy. Another message suggests that Intimacy can be dangerous to one's sexual identity by creating a weak and ineffective personality.

Another bias is that men who are comfortable with sharing their emotional selves and who enjoy closeness are effeminate. It is believed, erroneously, that these men have less control in their lives and are not powerful enough to assume positions of authority. This is not unlike the common bias that women are too emotional to play effectively in the game of life.

Women also remain confused and struggle with their need for Intimacy. Often, society has a bias that ties Intimacy to nurturing, thus making it more acceptable for women than for men to be Intimate but only as it relates to taking care of others. This supports the bias that women are the nurturers and caretakers, never encouraging them to become Intimate with themselves.

The necessity to be trusting and even vulnerable at times to meet their Intimacy needs creates conflict for some women. They fear that if they become too vulnerable or too trusting they risk being ridiculed or injured in some way. This conflict results from the large numbers of women who have not been protected from injurious or demeaning acts by either their families or society. Such confusion blocks women from confronting their need for Intimacy.

Men also suffer because of this bias and continue to deny their need for healthy vulnerability and trusting relationships. For men, feelings of vulnerability and closeness imply a weakness that threatens their overall identity and success.

So often it's difficult for either gender to be comfortable feeling vulnerable, being open and sharing because messages from their past and gender bias encourage both to remain closed, guarded and unemotional.

Intimacy still remains a mystery in an otherwise progressive and sophisticated society. Although we know more about Intimacy than ever before, many people remain confused and uncomfortable with it.

Without exhibiting any curiosity, many people have accepted biases about Intimacy that constrict its needful and exciting purpose and meaning. Women and men have not challenged this specific need nearly as much as they should. Making a choice to trust yourself, to be vulnerable and to expose your deep desires, wants and needs is a healthy way to develop respect.

The Solitude Need

Think about a time of day when you are typically completely alone, a time when you are with your own thoughts and feelings. For some, such a time may only happen early in the morning before a busy day begins. For others, it might be in the evening when the day is winding down. But many people avoid having *any* time alone.

Most people don't give much thought to Solitude and don't consider it important to their quality of life. Our society is filled with pressures and expectations and does not lend itself to cultivating inner peace and insight. With our materialistic establishment, the emphasis has mostly been on the external rather than the internal. So it's not surprising that the majority of men and women find difficulty relating to their need for Solitude.

A solitary time can be a time of rejuvenation. It's a time to be free, to enjoy being alone with yourself. A time to think your own thoughts and a time to feel your own

~ ~

feelings. Whether these thoughts and feelings are good or bad isn't the question. More importantly, the questions are: Do you let yourself have these times? Do you know the art of creating these solitary moments?

Most of us don't! Most of us fear Solitude because we look on it as a type of isolation and loneliness. Or worse yet, we're so afraid to be alone with our private thoughts and feelings that we avoid Solitude and cheat ourselves out of an opportunity to learn our innermost secrets. Out of fear or denial, some of us fill our days with busy activities, while others find diversions through work or friends.

Many of the women and men I interviewed told me how much they prided themselves on their ability to stay busy and involved, thereby ignoring their own internal voices. They believed these internal voices or their internal feelings would hinder them in some way.

Yet when questioned further, they weren't sure why they felt this way. None of them had given any thought to the amount of intimate information they were denying themselves by not satisfying this need. They weren't in touch with how these internal messages were pertinent to their behavior.

The ability to delve, to be introspective, is a skill that puts you in touch with your personal thoughts and feelings. It helps increase your self-knowledge and self-understanding. This is a necessity if you wish to experience yourself in an authentic and intimate way — a way that is honest, caring, loving, powerful and effective.

A Man Who Learned About Solitude

Through personal experience and struggle, Paul learned the difference between his need for Solitude and the life of isolation he had created. His isolation wasn't the peaceful time of introspection he had anticipated. Instead, it increased his anger, added to his depression and confused his thoughts and feelings.

Originally, Paul struggled to balance his life. He left his job after a long period of dissatisfaction. His second marriage ended and his relationships with his adult children were not pleasurable.

"I was angry and disappointed, and I just wanted to be left alone. I had enough money to kick back for a while, but little did I know how unfortunate this was going to be. I moved to a new area, away from everyone and everything I knew. My intention, I told myself, was to start over. This time I was going to have it my way—whatever that meant. Weeks ran into months, months into three years. I was nearly broke and as unhappy as I can ever remember being. I had a vague realization that I was drinking heavily."

Paul told me that with persistence from an old friend and some professional help, he began some serious soul searching. He was encouraged to see the positive influence of Solitude and how to use it for increased insight. Through the process of therapy and using GEM as a guide, he began taking more responsibility for his choices. He discovered that much could be gained by not blaming others for his unhappiness. He realized that being alone, when it's a conscious choice made for the sake of learning, is never negative. The nurturing and revelations provided by Solitude are necessary for the continued development of self-confidence and creativity.

Solitude offered Paul information, choices and self-understanding, while his state of isolation had kept him stuck in negativity, shutting him off from positive introspection. Isolation never enhances one's opinion of oneself

~ ~

and doesn't lead to meaningful interactions. Instead it stifles communication.

As Paul's awareness increased, it became easier for him to make a shift in his thinking. His new thoughts allowed him to reevaluate his Solitude needs and meet these needs constructively. His self-destructive behavior diminished. His world began to change in ways that let him emotionally reinvest in himself and others. Solitude became a major contributor in Paul's success, but as he pointed out, "It was only after I began satisfying my need for a deeper understanding of myself that I started to reap the benefits of spending time with myself. I simply didn't see how my isolation was hurting me. In fact, I had never given the word or the feeling any thought. I guess for me, Solitude and isolation were the same. And as long as that was my perception, I continued to overlook what Solitude could do for me.

"Now, my moments of Solitude give me the opportunity to explore aspects of my personality that I'm unaware of.

"Prior to my therapy, I didn't look inside for my answers. I only looked outward to my world and the people in it. I often felt miserable, and these were the times I withdrew into myself. I would shut down my feelings and shut out those closest to me. I never shared my feelings or my thoughts. Looking back, I can see the futility in that non-communication. This behavior left me frustrated most of the time. On some level, I was always angry.

"But once I satisfied my need for Solitude, I found that going to that quiet place within to sort through my thoughts and feelings was adventurous. It was in that Solitary place that I learned to trust my own answers. It was during a time of Solitude that I gained the most control over my life and was able to plan for my future success."

Paul is to be commended for his willingness to challenge and confront his behavior in order to improve his life conditions. Many people fail to acknowledge their needs or to challenge their behavior. They continue to run away from their disappointments or their emotional pain. They isolate themselves or avoid the place within where their truth lies, their Intimate Self. Their personalities often deteriorate because they lose the enthusiasm and positive energy that promote a zest for a quality life.

Standing Alone

There is no guarantee that you will always have someone to stand beside you, to comfort you, to care for you or to look out for you. If you haven't already been in this position, you may not understand how important it is to know how to stand alone. The ability to stand alone when necessary, without experiencing yourself as lost or out of control, is a positive strength, that can enable you to operate with confidence and self-assurance.

Circumstances such as divorce or the death of a loved one can impose aloneness on you. When this occurs, initial feelings of isolation, loneliness and emotional pain are to be expected. However, even under these unwanted circumstances, following a certain amount of time, feelings of isolation need to be replaced with Solitude. This is the only way to get on with your life. If you remain stuck in isolation, your entire personality and lifestyle may suffer.

Determining the Difference

If you often feel unhappy, depressed, lonely, angry, agitated or apathetic, chances are you are emotionally or

~ ~

physically isolated. You may even be both. If you more often feel competent, centered, self-assured and confident, you probably have been using time alone to meet your need for Solitude.

Let your behavior be another clue for determining the difference between isolation and Solitude. If your behavior is destructive in any way, and you recognize that you push people away or create disharmony around yourself, then you can be relatively sure that your need for Solitude is not being met appropriately.

If your behavior is positive and creates harmony, you probably know the importance of Solitude and choose to take time for solitary moments whenever you find it necessary or helpful.

Solitude plays an important role in our maturation process. It gives us the opportunity to experience the evolution of our Intimate self. So whether Solitude is your choice or whether it's forced upon you through circumstances beyond your control, the secret is to recognize it as a time for growth and a time to become in touch with yourself.

Remember, if you are comfortable with Solitude the chances of your becoming isolated are significantly decreased.

A Woman Who Was Forced
to Understand Solitude

Ruth's husband left her unexpectedly. When she first came into counseling, she was feeling confused and lonely. She was afraid and unsure of how to get on with her life. Initially, Ruth needed to give herself permission to mourn her loss and to work through her loneliness, her pain and her anger. But the time came when it was vital for her to move on and to challenge her new status. Ruth needed to meet her need for Solitude.

Once Ruth moved beyond the pain, she began to explore untapped emotional strengths. Although life wasn't the same as she once knew it, she learned that change can be positive. In Solitude, Ruth was able to unearth insights involving her capabilities and competence.

Ruth is an example of someone who learned to turn what appeared to be negative into something positive. Much to her surprise, she found a level of contentment that she never knew existed. This unexpected gain is not unusual because people generally discover interesting things about themselves when they take a positive approach to life. Solitude offers a place within you that addresses your competence.

Biases and Prejudices Attached to Solitude

I found while training corporate managers and supervisors that the majority of these bright women and men were in conflict with their Intimacy and Solitude needs. Many of them scored the lowest in this GEM relationship on the Personality Dimension Scale.

Most were not shocked by their lower Intimacy scores, but they were surprised to learn how Solitude was dependent on Intimacy and vice versa. Solitude was more repressed and less accepted as a valuable need in these managers' lives. They questioned not only its importance to them personally, but its relevance to their workplace.

As the discussions and role plays developed during these GEM workshops, it became increasingly apparent how little Solitude was used as a viable tool to enhance employee relations. For the most part, even the customary coffee breaks were not used for relaxation and rejuvenation. Instead, they were a continuation of work-related conversation and interaction. Primarily, this was due to the lack of knowledge people had regarding their Solitude need.

Both women and men have operated out of a bias or belief that too much time spent thinking about themselves is negative and unproductive. Can you ever remember hearing statements like these:

"Why don't you focus on something other than yourself?"

"When was the last time you thought of someone other than yourself?"

"Quit feeling sorry for yourself!"

"Do you think you are the only one who has problems?"

These types of statements are not uncommon. They greatly affect us when we buy into them and adopt them into our belief system. As children, these types of messages had a negative impact on us.

We tend to believe it's bad to concentrate on ourselves. We often feel guilty when we turn our thoughts inward, so we frequently dismiss the validity of our thoughts and feelings. In doing so, we do not adequately meet our need for Solitude.

Many of us think that taking time for ourselves means we are selfish, vain or self-centered. But clearly, we need to turn inward and focus on ourselves to meet our need for Solitude. Women who operate out of the bias that their main purpose in life is to be the caretakers or nurturers of others find themselves in great conflict when they try to meet their personal need for Solitude.

~ ~

Most of the biases and prejudices connected to Solitude are subtle. Research and literature relating to Solitude are scarce. Yet, throughout history, there have been and still remain cultures like the Buddhists, for example, whose teachings focus on Solitude as a way to develop and master their internal strength.

Solitude and Your Health

Stress is a serious problem in our society. An increasing number of people suffer from various illnesses due to the buildup of life's stresses. Your ability to meet your need for Solitude in a healthy and consistent way can offset the amount of bad stress affecting you.

When you create time for Solitude or elect to let your alone times be solitary rather than isolating and depressing, your needs and wants can become positive, obtainable goals controlled by you. In general your life improves, your level of stress decreases, and your overall health is less at risk.

A Woman at Risk

Christine is an overachiever who constantly felt pressure to prove herself. She never knew her father, and her mother worked very hard to provide a living for herself and Christine. Work kept Christine's mother away from home most of the time, so Christine was raised by babysitters and attended numerous day-care programs. Her emotional needs were not sufficiently met. Therefore she grew up feeling cheated, not cared about and hell-bent on proving herself worthwhile. Christine took on school, a career and her family as though each minute was her last, and she insisted on being in control of everything.

As the years went by, Christine felt more and more burdened by her choices. Her messages from the past far outweighed her present-day personal needs. So she continued to push herself even when she was exhausted. As a result, her stress level soared, and soon she was at great risk. One day, Christine found herself unable to get out of bed.

Making the rounds of many doctors, she underwent numerous tests, but no physical evidence of any disease or illness could be noted. Her symptoms could not be explained. Yet she remained unable to function on a normal level, and was bedridden for three months. During these months Christine concluded that her unrealistic need to prove herself was destroying her emotionally and physically. Solitude became Christine's avenue to health.

We all have a tendency to take our need for Solitude much too lightly. Like Christine, we often wait until we're faced with a crisis or serious physical symptoms before acknowledging this need and adopting it into our day-to-day living.

Solitude empowers you through the experience of your own competence. It helps you to handle situations with self-assurance and inner confidence.

Solitude is your opportunity to be with yourself in a healing, meditative, and creative way.

Meeting this need will help you maintain a harmonious life.

Chapter Nine

Intimacy/Solitude Relationship: Characteristics

~ ~

People who are secure and feel good about themselves understand the importance of internal balance. They cherish their Solitude and enjoy the different degrees of Intimacy. They know how to create internal balance between their Intimacy and Solitude needs. Because all six GEM needs are interdependent, it's critical to your effectiveness to create a reasonable balance between all of the needs.

To be effective, you must build rapport with people. Building good rapport is a positive communication skill that leads to good social skills. Many people ignore the value of good social skills, so they don't know how to make others feel comfortable and important. We naturally look up to those who can make themselves understood, and we tend to trust and admire those who present themselves well.

When you create balance between Intimacy and Solitude, you can expect your personal and professional involvement with others to become far more pleasurable and powerful.

This second GEM relationship builds from the foundation you originally laid when you met your need for Self-Love and Self-Power. It is a continuation and extension of your personal growth. Each step you take to create internal balance between Intimacy and Solitude builds the personality characteristics that command respect.

To have insight into your behavior and attitudes is not enough. You also need to know how to use this insight when you connect with your external world. This is a critical step toward the evolvement of your personality and your personal success.

Chances are you have already developed a certain amount of balance between your Intimacy and Solitude need. But this balance can be increased by expanding your knowledge of these two needs and stretching yourself like never before. That's what balance is all about, the decision to stretch yourself beyond your present comfort zone to gain something more positive in your life. Your potential is limitless, so take this opportunity to increase your experience of both Intimacy and Solitude, and create for yourself a better balance in this relationship. The outcome will be positive. Acknowledging and meeting your need for balance between Intimacy and Solitude is always a win-win proposition.

An Activity in Solitude

Close the door. If anyone bothers you, ask them to please excuse you. If they don't, politely ask them to leave, then shut the door and LOCK IT! Get into a comfortable position and try to relax. Give yourself permission (for just a few minutes) not to worry. Take some long deep breaths and let yourself feel every part of your body letting go and relaxing. Now go inward to your Intimate self and listen to what your inner voice has to say about how you meet your need for Intimacy and Solitude. Ask your inner self the following questions; you may want to write down your answers:

1. When was the last time I trusted another person enough to share something meaningful with her or him?
2. How good do I feel about the relationships in my life?
3. When was the last time I spent time alone and enjoyed myself?
4. In the past week, what situation made me feel competent? What action did I take to create this feeling?

As you ponder these questions, be aware of any feelings that stir within you. Try not to get caught in your thoughts, and try not to think about what you feel. Just feel. Let yourself enjoy this time. When you are ready to return, we will continue. If you are feeling good, don't rush yourself. This is what Solitude is all about, so experience it. You will want to create balance between these two needs once you acknowledge your need for Intimacy in your life, and once you understand that your need for Solitude is essential to your independence. Internal balance between Intimacy and Solitude can serve you well. It engenders greater sensitivity and objectivity.

As I explained earlier, a person might stop short of experiencing deep levels of Intimacy and pleasurable times of Solitude for many reasons. But regardless of the reasons, the outcome usually is the same — damage and restriction to the individual's personality. If you have remained at an emotional level that never quite fills a void within you or

~ ~

leaves you feeling inadequate, this choice was made from old information about yourself versus new and updated information. It's crucial to increase your self-awareness to protect yourself from making the dangerous mistake of not creating a deeper experience of these two needs. Repeat the following sentences to increase your self-awareness:

"As a responsible adult, I am the only person interpreting the information I receive. Any information that I don't like I can challenge or I can change. It's in my control!" Try to repeat this statement several times a day. This is a good way to remind yourself that you have choices and options in your life.

People Whose Intimacy/Solitude Needs Are in Balance

People internally balanced between Intimacy and Solitude bond with others in a meaningful and comfortable way. They communicate with self-confidence and ease and listen with an attentive ear. Their competence creates a harmonious atmosphere.

- ***They are good communicators.***

Their communication skills have developed out of an honest and positive approach to life. They are not afraid to share, which encourages others to share in return. They are direct and assertive, and they enjoy involvement.

- ***They are perceptive.***

They have a genuine interest in people. They are in touch with their internal voices and listen to what their intuition tells them. They trust this internal information.

- ***They are introspective.***

They turn inward as a way to examine their thoughts

and feelings. They are subjective and contemplative. They compare internal information with external information.

- ***They are trustworthy.***

They don't have ulterior motives because they are comfortable and secure within themselves. They have no desire to get ahead at the cost of another person.

- ***They are good observers.***

Their ability to observe comes from their level of patience and natural curiosity. They need not always be in the spotlight.

- ***They are open.***

It is easy to be open when you are secure about yourself. Open people are sharing. They understand the importance of different viewpoints, and they enjoy the differences.

- ***They work well alone.***

They have an internalized independence that does not require the approval or acknowledgment of others. They know the difference between isolation and Solitude.

Many people try to achieve equal balance between their Intimacy and Solitude needs because they want healthy relationships. They appreciate who they are as individuals, and they respect the uniqueness of others. They understand how important it is to broaden their judgment about people and life in their attempt to live life to its fullest.

They recognize the value in creating internal balance between these needs, and they take the necessary risks to make this balance happen. They are not afraid of negative responses; they welcome such responses as another way to learn about how they are perceived.

~ ~

People Whose Intimacy/Solitude Needs Are Out of Balance

Women and men who have not created balance between Intimacy and Solitude are often fearful and inwardly stuck in a negative place. They are afraid to be open and sharing. They are often rigid in their thinking and operate with blinders on as a way to protect themselves. In general, they experience anxious feelings or feelings of insecurity.

It's not unusual for these people to be in conflict in their relationships at work and at home. Unfortunately, they often lack the ability to be honest enough with themselves to recognize their need to change. In most cases, they view any dissension or problems as the fault of the situation or the other person. Hopefully, they will happen upon a situation or person that forces them to take a second look at themselves. If they avoid the risk of taking a more honest look and refuse to challenge themselves, their negative behavior probably will continue as their usual mode of operation.

People Whose Intimacy Fulfillment Is Low or Misdirected

- ***They are afraid of closeness.***
  They create distance between themselves and others as a form of self-protection. Because they frequently experience feelings of insecurity and distrust, they are afraid to risk being vulnerable.
- ***They build limited relationships.***
  Intimacy either frightens them or is unfamiliar.

They're not open because they fear they won't be accepted for who they are. Others are unable to be involved with them on a deep or meaningful level.

- ***They have difficulty identifying their feelings.***

They have not learned how to turn inward to their Intimate Self, so they are not clear about what they are feeling or why they are feeling it.

- ***They lack authenticity.***

Because they lack information and clarity about themselves, they remain out of touch with certain aspects of their personality. They lack a "realness" that contributes to their feeling uncomfortable and which creates discomfort in others. Their presentation of themselves is often stiff.

- ***They are afraid of honest self-disclosure.***

This limits their ability to probe deep within themselves as a way to become better acquainted with their deeper truths. So they remain rigid in their thinking and lack clues to their real needs or wants. Their level of personal sharing is highly selective and restrictive.

- ***They are afraid to trust.***

When people aren't in touch with their feelings, they often make poor choices that lower their self-confidence. Low self-confidence can lead to distrust of oneself, which leads to distrust of others.

- ***They create disharmony.***

In an effort to remain safe, they distance themselves from others with behavior that is negative and unpleasant. This behavior can range from coldness and rudeness to openly hostility and abusiveness.

- ***They are guarded.***

They communicate on a superficial level. This protects them from personal exposure, and provides another way to remain distant.

~ ~

- ***They feel cheated.***

A lack of Intimacy leaves a person feeling empty and cheated. Often these people carry a chip on their shoulder or become bitter.

A Woman Whose Intimacy Fulfillment Was Low

Pat sought counseling to improve the relationships in her life. She arrived at her first appointment somewhat apprehensive, but eager to change. This forty-six-year-old woman was involved in a relationship that was neither practical nor pleasurable. Although she described herself as an independent woman who took pride in her ability to make decisions, her attempts to end this relationship had been unsuccessful.

Discussing the past relationships in her life, Pat said that each lacked the closeness she wanted. "I was thirty-one when I divorced my husband. Our marriage wasn't good from the beginning. We co-existed for the six years we were together. He cheated on me, and most of the time I knew it. But after the second or third time, it didn't seem to hurt as bad, so I just ignored it. But I also ignored him."

During Pat's therapy, she discovered that she had never seen her parents display any expression of Intimacy. She said, "Mom and Dad stayed together, but I never understood why. Their marriage was a fake in many ways.

"To the outside world, our family looked good. We did all of the right things. We took family vacations, went out to dinner together, lived in a nice house in a nice neighborhood and went to family reunions. It all appeared fine. But it wasn't fine.

~ ~

"My folks either fought with one another or ignored one another. They were never kind to each other unless they were in front of other people. My brother and I walked on eggshells, never knowing what the mood in the house would be.

"On occasion, when Dad drank too much, he became affectionate and this made Mom angry. In fact, those were the only times I can remember my Dad being affectionate. Those times made me feel uncomfortable.

"My personal life was pretty mundane until I graduated from college and landed a job with a good company. It took me just two years to reach management level and then my life was reasonably happy and content. I had my own place and my independence. Unlike when I was growing up, my life felt peaceful.

"However, I didn't date much, and when I did, I was uncomfortable and insecure. I had women friends but I wasn't real close to any of them. I guess you could say I was a loner."

As Pat examined her relationships with both men and women, she recognized how superficial they were. She didn't let anyone get too close. Openness was uncomfortable for Pat. She especially kept her distance from men and only dated those who were incapable of closeness. A perfect example of this was her ex-husband, whom she couldn't trust to risk closeness.

Pat's tolerance for Intimacy with herself or anyone else was tentative. Her present relationship was with a man who also couldn't give Pat Intimacy. He was married and unable to offer her any commitment or emotional security. But luckily for her, this was the relationship that forced Pat to confront herself. It caused her enough internal conflict to bring her into therapy.

~ ~

Challenging her past and the old messages she had received about relationships, closeness, friendship and other aspects of Intimacy, Pat began to probe deeper. As her therapy progressed, she ended her relationship and allowed herself to feel the pain of the loss. She reached out to others and shared bits and pieces of herself. With each success, she shared bigger, more meaningful parts of herself. Eventually, Pat met a man who was warm, self-assured and available. As their relationship grew, Pat invited more Intimacy into her life.

"I was so afraid to open up to this person. But over and over, he said or did something that showed me how much he trusted me. I started to relax. I wanted to give something back. And of course, through therapy I had learned a great deal about myself. Now I had a chance to put all that I had learned to work."

Pat continued to build her relationship with this man as well as her relationships with others. Her journey into her Intimate Self revealed many buried emotions. As each emotion exposed itself, she became more aware of the void in her life and her increasing need for Intimacy. Not all stories have a happy ending, but Pat is now married and enjoying her new roles as a loving partner and as a step-parent.

People Whose Solitude Fulfillment Is Low or Misdirected

- *They avoid their deeper feelings.*
  They are external people rather than internal people.
- *They isolate themselves.*
  Many are emotionally injured, which causes them to

feel angry, bitter or resentful. They perceive themselves as lonely. Unfortunately, they create an environment that reinforces this perception.

- *They have limited social skills.*

They don't comfortably tolerate deep levels of communication, so their interactions are limited and often superficial. They experience aloneness as loneliness.

- *They don't know the difference between isolation and Solitude.*

They tend to withdraw. Generally, this is due to discomfort, fear or other internal uneasiness.

- *They lack good support systems.*

Because they've cut themselves off from significant relationships, their means of emotional support is limited. This deficit encourages psychological deprivation and discourages closeness. Many of them suffer from substance abuse. Solitude offers an individual a sense of inner peace and internalized competence. When the Solitude need is not met, chances become greater for a person to cover up her/his unsettled emotions with a numbing substance.

- *They are suspicious of people's motives.*

This encourages withdrawal, isolation and misinterpretation, which inhibit positive growth in relationships.

- *They deny their Intimacy needs.*

This creates loneliness and decreases meaningful involvement with others. Their rationale for what is lacking in their life is distorted or justified by their acceptance of superficial relationships.

- *Their health is at risk.*

Physical and emotional contact with others is necessary to survive the stresses of life. To adopt a healthy attitude, everyone needs to feel wanted, needed and valued. Positive attitudes are positive energy and natural healers.

~ ~

A Man Who Needed Solitude

Jim spent the greater part of his fifty-two years creating his empire. His initial request when he came into therapy was to learn how to make the relationships in his life run more smoothly. On some level, he understood that he wasn't enjoying any feelings of closeness with his family and he felt sad about this. He was unaware of exactly what prevented this closeness.

When asked to explain further, he said, "My wife always complains about me and is forever letting me know how I don't spend enough time with her and the kids. She feels that I neglect her and she insists that I'm insensitive.

"My kids, on the other hand, don't seem to care if I'm around or not, except when it affects them. They enjoy all that I have to give, but they really don't appreciate it. When I think about it, I can't remember the last time one of them asked me how I was. I'm always home on weekends, and truthfully, I can't wait to get back to my office. That's where the action is and that's where I feel the best.

"There's no question in my mind that my wife and my kids don't have a clue as to what it has taken me to get where I am. They just reap the benefits and count on me to take care of everything. I don't feel appreciated, and I don't feel concern from any of them."

Jim went on to describe how hard he had worked throughout his life to reach his goals. His story was impressive. It was apparent he had driven himself to reach his present status. Yet, now that he was financially secure and his business could be maintained by competent employees, Jim felt lonely, unsure about his future and estranged from his family.

He was feeling what many men feel when they stop

long enough to reevaluate their lives, empty or subtly discontent.

Jim needed time to become introspective. He needed time to speculate and contemplate, time to sort through his thoughts and feelings and explore the purpose of his life. It was time for him to confront what he thought was missing from his life. And when he discovered what was missing, he needed to understand what he had or hadn't done to create it. Jim needed to learn how to turn inward and listen for his answers. He needed Solitude. It was time for Jim to feel and understand emotions that he had never allowed himself to identify.

It's not unusual for both men and women to get caught up in their ambition and ignore their emotional selves.

Jim gained insight into his relationships. "As I started to work in my therapy, I began to recognize how much I distanced myself from people — all people, not just my family. I'm friendly enough, but I've never taken the time to develop real friendships.

I've always been on the run trying to accomplish one thing or another. It never occurred to me that I was hurting my family in any way. I always believed that if I provided my family with financial security and gave them the better things in life they would know how much I loved them. I sure as hell gave them more than *I* ever had. I really resented my wife's complaints over the years, and I guess I blamed her for my children's indifferent attitudes. Now I know that my absence from home and my unrealistic drive came from an old belief system about my role as a man."

After some self-investigation, Jim's understanding of himself changed. He was shocked to discover how many choices he had made in his life without first having an understanding of his own patterns of behavior. He was amazed at how these patterns of behavior had affected those choices. Through Jim's willingness to learn more about what made him tick, he uncovered more information about himself.

Jim ended our final session by saying, "I thank God for my choice to examine my life because, in doing so, I also learned that my fear of closeness was another real enemy."

Solitude is one of the best medicines for stress. It's your internal cure for negativity. During this quiet time, you can address any emotion or internal conflict that may be bothering you. It's only out of a lack of knowledge that you remain unaware of what behavior is blocking your effectiveness. Solitude offers a time to learn more about yourself. Remember, you will only resist change when you're unsure about how to replace negative behavior with new and positive behavior.

Solitude gives you the time out to contemplate and fantasize about anything you desire. As a gift to yourself, rethink your need for Solitude and increase your awareness of its purpose in your life.

Chapter Ten

Intimacy/Solitude Relationship: Key Action Steps

~ ~

As you approach the final destination of your journey through Intimacy and Solitude, experiment with your Intimate Self. Turn inward and probe deep; investigate any hidden feelings or emotions that you have been ignoring. Quietly sit back and question yourself about how you meet your needs for Intimacy and Solitude. If this is difficult, the following activity should be helpful.

Instructions: Let your thoughts drift back in time and explore your history as it relates to Intimacy and Solitude. Get in touch with the old messages surrounding these two needs. Take a few deep breaths and allow yourself to feel the oxygen penetrating your body. As you relax, try to create a picture of yourself as a child. What age are you in this image? Now try to picture yourself at even a younger age.

On paper, write down your answers to the following questions:

1. Did I experience Intimacy while growing up?

~ ~

2. When did I first become aware of needing Solitude?
3. What is my definition of Intimacy and Solitude?
4. Am I comfortable with physical closeness?
5. Am I comfortable with emotional closeness?
6. Do I feel comfortable sharing my thoughts and feelings with another person?
7. Do I stop long enough to identify my feelings or do I ignore them?
8. Am I content when I am alone?
9. Does being alone make me feel lonely?
10. How do I react to emotional pain?
11. How honest am I with myself?
12. Am I willing to be open and honest with others?
13. Do I isolate myself when I feel troubled or depressed?
14. Do I have lasting relationships?
15. Do I enjoy meeting new people and doing new things?
16. Do I like to learn new things about myself?
17. Do I listen to others as a way to learn about myself?
18. Do I take the types of risks that give me new experiences of myself?
19. Do I like others to see the real me?
20. Do I need others' approval to feel okay about myself?
21. Do I feel independent and competent?
22. When was the last time I read a self-help book?
23. Do I like change?

Your answers should help you focus on any pertinent feelings and issues you may have with Intimacy and Solitude. Think of your answers as indicators; they point toward the various reasons you may hold yourself back from creating balance in this second GEM relationship.

Be honest in your self-disclosure; try to be objective enough to recognize any contradictions in your life that you may be acting out through your behavior. People often say one thing but do another. Or they feel a particular way but cover up that feeling with the opposite feeling. For example, some parents speak words of love to their child, but their actions are unloving. Another example might be a time when you felt sad, but denied the feeling or replaced it with another feeling such as anger or humor. Perhaps you bury certain feelings completely and convince yourself you feel nothing.

When you separate your thoughts from your feelings, your authentic self becomes compromised or disguised. This type of incongruity has a negative effect on your total behavior. When this happens, your thoughts and feelings are not in sync. Your words don't match your actions and your entire emotional response system is out of balance. It's extremely important to become conscious of such contradictions in your life. They play an important role in how effective you will be.

Before moving on to the key action steps, look back over your test scores from Chapter Three, then study the notes you made about Intimacy and Solitude and how they fit into your present life. Think of them as you study the following summary of the major points made in this chapter.

I consider the Intimacy and Solitude relationship to be the most challenging of the three relationships in the GEM model. I believe this is the most difficult relationship to explore because it taps into one's vulnerability. It can feel disquieting to be open and vulnerable. Internal discomfort

~ ~

can discourage you from wanting to get in touch with your Intimate Self. But if you choose to create internal balance between Intimacy and Solitude, you must be willing to confront what keeps you misdirected or out of balance in this relationship. Creating internal balance between your need for Intimacy and Solitude will enhance the quality of the relationships in your life. Your awareness and insight will increase.

This GEM relationship encourages your involvement with others. You will have your most positive experience with Intimacy when you become comfortable enough within yourself to learn from, and enjoy interacting with other people. It is healthy to form meaningful and lasting relationships. These relationships bring purpose and support to your life.

GEM invites you to continue confronting any fears that plague you. It encourages you to examine whatever hesitations that you may have, and it teaches you to get on with the fun of living — living a style of life that offers more happiness and commands more respect than you ever imagined possible. Don't take your need for Intimacy and Solitude lightly. Your ability to meet these two needs adequately is of critical importance to your success.

Intimacy/Solitude Key Action Steps

How to Satisfy Your Need for Intimacy in Your Personal Life:

- *Step 1. Acknowledge your Intimate Self.*
  Your first key action step toward meeting your need for Intimacy is to acknowledge that you are a person capable of Intimacy. Deep within you is a place where you

~ ~

can go to embrace your feelings and your true self. Get acquainted with this place by accepting it as part of you, that wonderful *authentic* you.

- ***Step 2. Trust your Intimate Self.***

You have an internal mechanism (your built-in radar) that operates in your best interest. You can be in touch with your Intimate Self simply by turning inward. Listen. Try to hear what those deeper feelings are saying. Don't push them away or hide them from yourself. They belong to you, they're valid, and they're feelings that give you truer information about yourself and others.

- ***Step 3. Examine your personal definition of Intimacy.***

Think about the questions you answered in the beginning of this chapter. Did you perhaps notice that some of your answers were vague or that you couldn't answer some of them at all?

Now, compare my definition of Intimacy in Chapter Eight with *your* definition of Intimacy. Judge for yourself how close the two definitions are.

- ***Step 4. Understand the joy of vulnerability.***

Think of something personal, something that no one could know about you unless you told them. Can you imagine telling this to someone? Who would you pick, and why?

After you complete this mental exercise, try it out in the real world. This time, pick someone you didn't name and try to tell that person.

Recognize through this exercise that even when you're vulnerable and exposing new information about yourself, you're still in control. Vulnerability is your choice. You can pick and choose when and with whom to be vulnerable.

~ ~

- *Step 5. Learn to rely on your instincts and judgment.*

People who trust themselves rely on their instincts and judgment. They benefit the most and reap the most pleasure from their Intimate Selves. If you find you've made a mistake, chalk it up to a good learning experience and try again. With enough attempts, you will succeed. Relying on yourself is the road to self-confidence and independence.

- *Step 6. Get intimate with your "whole" self.*

Know your body. You can be your own best diagnostician if you pay attention to your body and the messages it sends to you through physical, spiritual and mental signals. Learn to listen for these messages.

Most people treat their heads, their bodies and their emotions as three separate entities, never recognizing the importance for these three miracles to work together to create wholeness.

Also, be willing to acquaint yourself with your body by touching yourself all over and learning your different responses to each sensation or feeling.

Being comfortable with your own body is just another aspect of Intimacy. Be willing to enjoy touching yourself. Be gentle and caring and always find something good about the way your body feels and looks. Understand how your body and its emotions may or may not be matching what your head is thinking. Ask yourself, "How often does this type of contradiction happen?" The more aware you become of this internal conflict, the better chance you'll have to correct whatever is out of sync. When you operate holistically, you will reap the benefits of functioning from a centered position, with a feeling of control and internalized harmony. This is the only way to operate if you want a harmonious and effective life.

- ***Step 7. Learn to forgive yourself.***

All of us have said or done things that make us feel ashamed or guilty. It's time to forgive yourself. Sit alone and write down anything you've done that is causing you regret or emotional pain. Once you have made your list, take one situation at a time and forgive yourself for this thought, word or deed. It's essential that you believe and accept your words of forgiveness, or you will not feel freed from your pain. Remember, such negative feelings of guilt, resentment, anger or sadness are unnecessary stumbling blocks that get in the way of your happiness.

- ***Step 8. Look and listen for the unfamiliar you.***

Don't be so sure that you know everything there is to know about yourself. Learn to be your own best detective and investigate the hidden parts of your personality. You can do this by trying new things and then experiencing your responses to them. Here are some examples: Read a type of book that you never thought would be interesting to you, or see a movie that you would otherwise pass up. Try a new craft or take up a hobby.

The secret to exploring the hidden you is to do things that are unfamiliar and to become conscious of their impact. Try to do at least one new thing a week for one month. At the end of the month you will have new information about yourself. You also will have stretched yourself further, recognizing even more of your unlimited potential.

- ***Step 9. Check your pace.***

Your level of emotional comfort is important and deserves your respect. Be patient with yourself, allow yourself to go at your own pace. Don't try to pace yourself with someone else. Any discomfort you experience during the process of change is normal, but if you allow the discomfort to overwhelm you, your attempts to grow will be unsuccessful. So keep a check on your pace. Take this personal responsibility seriously.

How to Satisfy Your Need for Intimacy in Your Work Life:

- ### *Step 1. Get involved.*

If you are shy or unsure as to how to reach out to others, begin by involving yourself in a project, sport or activity that requires more than just you to participate. If you are not feeling some emotional discomfort when you do this, chances are you have taken the easy way out and found something that was safe for you.

Stretch yourself; try something that has some emotional risk attached to it.

After you have succeeded at this, *stretch* even further. Go to dinner by yourself and find someone in the restaurant you can invite to sit and eat with you or invite yourself to eat with them. Sounds painful? It's not as bad as you think. Try it. But remember, do this latter part of the exercise under safe conditions whether you are male or female, NEVER, NEVER leave the restaurant with this person nor give out personal information such as your address or phone number.

- ### *Step 2. Learn to let down your protective wall.*

It's time to slowly let down the protective layers of insulation we talked about and allow new people at work into your life. To do this, your work colleagues need the opportunity to get to know you better. This will require you sharing more personal information about yourself. Be selective about whom you choose to do this level of sharing with.

~ ~

WARNING: Many people, when they first try this key action step, pick the wrong kind of person to share their personal information with. This results in feelings of disappointment or emotional pain because the person may not handle the information sensitively. There are unconscious reasons why people make these inappropriate choices. It may be out of habit and a way to justify an old belief system or it may be a way to rationalize their continued resistance to change. Either way, it's an attempt to avoid Intimacy and remain emotionally safe.

So be cautious when you take this step because you want a success. You'll have fun doing this once you recognize how responsive people are to you and your invitations. Remember, most people really want to be friendly.

- ***Step 3. Learn to be available.***

Learn to be both physically and emotionally available to other people in your organization. People will automatically reach out to you if you send out signals that are warm and inviting. An inviting signal can be as simple as a warm smile. Don't expect Intimacy in your life without being available.

- ***Step 4. Learn to make good eye contact.***

People who make good eye contact when they talk or listen make others feel more appreciated. People will feel that you are interested in them. This lays a foundation for good communication, which is one of the major steps to Intimacy.

- ***Step 5. Learn to ask people questions about themselves.***

You cannot develop Intimacy in the workplace if you are not willing to take the time to really know someone. Ask appropriate questions. Never ask anything too personal or too threatening. But ask questions that show a genuine

~ ~

interest in that person. A good way to start is to ask more when a co-worker comments on his or her personal life.

- ### *Step 6. Learn to be patient.*

Intimacy doesn't develop overnight. It takes time to build the type of trust that encourages Intimacy, so be patient with both yourself and the other person. If someone is guarded or distant with you, chances are they are unsure about what level of Intimacy they wish to have. When you're patient, it gives that person time to make this important determination. It also gives both of you time to build trust with one another.

- ### *Step 7. Be sensitive to others' needs.*

When you are sensitive to another's needs, you help set the stage for a work relationship that is open and honest. This type of communication encourages Intimacy in the workplace.

- ### *Step 8. Learn how to create a harmonious work environment.*

To meet your need for Intimacy in your workplace, you must help create an environment that allows people to feel valued, comfortable and secure. Each person needs to take responsibility for creating this environment, and they need to make this contribution in an effective way.

Check this out by asking yourself the following questions:

1. Is my attitude pleasant at work?
2. Do I make it a point to say positive things to my co-workers?
3. Do I surprise my co-workers with occasional treats such as cookies or cake?
4. Do I give frequent compliments when they're earned or deserved?
5. Am I fair with the people I work with, and do I

~ ~

go out of my way to show my appreciation of them?

6. When was the last time I invited a co-worker to lunch?

7. When was the last time I made someone at work laugh?

8. When was the last time I offered my assistance without being asked?

If you could not answer "yes" to at least four out of the first five questions, and if, for questions 6, 7 and 8, your answer wasn't within the last month, you're not doing enough to increase your Intimacy at work. Try some of these things; you'll be surprised at how it can change your life.

- *Step 9. Help another learn.*

You can always find someone who can use help. Be there with words of encouragement and lend a helping hand. You'll feel good knowing you helped someone else.

- *Step 10. Take risks with people.*

Make it a point to reach out to someone in some way every day. Even if you feel uncomfortable doing this, take this risk and learn how much each person has to offer in his/her own unique way. When you increase Intimacy in the workplace, each day is far more enjoyable and worthwhile.

How to Satisfy Your Need for Solitude in Your Personal Life:

- *Step 1. Don't confuse Solitude with isolation.*

This confusion creates unhappiness. People who can't differentiate between the two cut themselves off from the warmth and caring of others. This can lead to bitterness, loneliness, hostility or other such negative feelings.

~ ~

- *Step 2. Take time out for yourself.*

When you know the difference between Solitude and isolation, you can see the positive value in taking time out for yourself. You can use this time for whatever personal project or form of relaxation you choose. It's a moment in time when you don't have to feel responsible for anything or anyone.

Try it — you'll like it!

- *Step 3. Learn to recognize what you enjoy.*

Search yourself for what you enjoy feeling, doing and being. This cannot be done when all of your time is structured in a rigid or compulsive way. When you're flexible, you open yourself up to new experiences.

- *Step 4. Make your time alone positive.*

Time with yourself can be positive and exciting if you approach it with curiosity and an adventurous attitude. Recognize that time with yourself is the best time for you to challenge yourself without disrupting anyone else.

- *Step 5. Learn to relax.*

Relaxing is vital to your mental, emotional and physical health. If it's difficult for you to relax, purchase some relaxation tapes and play one each night at bedtime. Learn to concentrate on your breathing. Oxygen helps the healing process, so it's important to bring this wonderful gas into your body. Each time you take a deep breath and exhale, notice how your body relaxes, soothing and calming you. Through conscious effort, make sure you breathe correctly throughout your day and evening to encourage relaxation.

- *Step 6. Be open to learning new things about yourself.*

When you go with Solitude rather than resisting, and allow yourself to enjoy it, you can learn new things about yourself. Solitude gives you a chance to look at the present you and to examine your current reality.

Looking at this present state objectively can open the door to new information about yourself. Start now to challenge the old messages from your past by asking yourself the following questions:

1. Do you agree with everything you were taught?
2. Do you live in the present with the same values and rules as you did growing up?
3. Have you stopped periodically and questioned how different you are from the people who raised you?
4. Have you made it okay to be different?
5. Have you re-evaluated your beliefs, opinions and values and looked for your truth?
6. If your truth, ideas and aspirations differ greatly from others, are you still willing to be your own person?
7. Do you try new things and listen to new ideas? We only learn new things about ourselves when we challenge who we currently are. It's nice to recognize that we can make positive change in our life at any time.

- ***Step 7. Confront any fears you may have.***

We all fear some things in life. Fear can stop you from positive experiences. Fear can paralyze your life to the extent that you may never recognize your full potential. Even unknown fear can be detected through symptoms such as anxiety, phobias or physical ailments. Use these signals to acknowledge your fears so you can work toward eliminating them. If you seem unable to accomplish this, seek psychotherapy or some form of counseling to guide and support you through this change.

~ ~

Whatever you do, don't settle and allow fear to control your life.

- *Step 8. Let yourself be introspective.*

Solitude is quiet time that affords you an opportunity to turn inward to your Intimate Self, to contemplate, speculate and become introspective. Whether you seek answers, a re-evaluation of your life or a plan for your future, learning how to be introspective is a way to deal with your deep truths. Through introspection, you can learn valuable information about yourself that will help you develop and grow spiritually. Only let surface what feels safe to you. You have control. Rome wasn't built in a day, and you don't need to grow overnight. So be patient, but enjoy the self-learning and awareness that comes out of introspection.

- *Step 10. Develop your intuitiveness.*

Each time you reach inside of yourself for the answers, you develop a keener level of your intuitiveness. As you practice each of the key action steps to increase Solitude in your personal life, you will come to understand yourself more fully. With this deeper understanding, you will automatically become more insightful and intuitive. This is just one of the many benefits you reap from Solitude.

How to Satisfy Your Need for Solitude at Work:

- *Step 1. Find comfort in working alone.*

Too often, people cannot work alone without feeling isolated or left out. It's important to be able to work by yourself when it's necessary. The ability to do a job by yourself without the assistance or approval of another person is a credit to your self-confidence and independence.

- ***Step 2. Learn to enjoy your Solitude at work.***

Take thirty minutes each day for contemplation and speculation. Use this time to increase your focus and to clear your mind of any clutter that gets in the way of being productive or creative.

- ***Step 3. Don't always feel you must be part of the group.***

It is not necessary always to be part of a team. When Solitude presents itself to you, recognize it as something positive rather than interpreting it as being odd man out.

- ***Step 4. Create a place at work that is quiet.***

Make it your responsibility to create a place at work where Solitude can be used positively, a quiet place to minimize stress.

- ***Step 5. Let others respect your privacy.***

Solitude is also a type of privacy. It is the type of privacy that is not secretive, but instead gives you the tranquility to think your own thoughts and experience or envision your own ideas. When the difference between privacy and secrecy is apparent, people respect it. Make sure your behavior clearly indicates this difference.

- ***Step 6. Let people know you can work alone.***

If you haven't had an opportunity to work in a solitary way, create it! If you work under someone, ask her or him for an assignment that will give you this opportunity. If you are self-employed, chances are you have already had this experience. Did you like it? If you answered "no," then create another opportunity, and, this time, do what you can to make it enjoyable.

- ***Step 7. Rearrange your work hours.***

If you're a manager or supervisor, try to schedule your work hours to allow you to begin an hour earlier than your

~ ~ ~ ~ ~ ~ ~ ~ ~ ~ ~ ~ ~ ~ ~ ~ ~ ~ ~ ~

subordinates. If you're not in a position to establish your own hours, ask your manager for flex-time. Most major companies will let you start and leave earlier than the regular shift.

An hour alone in the morning gives you a chance to plan your day properly without interruption as well as providing you with some time for needed introspection. Planning does not waste time. It permits you to save time in the long run by clarifying and simplifying your goals.

- *Step 8. Eat lunch alone at least two days a week.*

At work, it's important to maintain contacts with clients and colleagues. Eating lunch with others sometimes provides a good setting to help you accomplish that end. But it is equally important to give yourself some alone-time to think through the problems of the day and to plan the future. An excellent place to do this is at a pleasant, quiet restaurant. Don't forget to pencil in these fulfilling lunch dates in your calendar at the beginning of each week.

- *Step 9. Redecorate your office or work area.*

Most offices look barren and cold. They're designed to be functional, but a sterile environment disrupts Solitude and discourages the occasional introspection so necessary for survival in our fast-paced business world. Put balance into your work life by bringing in pleasant artwork or touches of home. Make your office or work environment warm and inviting, a place you normally associate with comfort and peace.

- *Step 10. Add time for yourself to business trips.*

When business demands an out-of-town trip, try to schedule the trip for the beginning or end of a week and add on part of the weekend for some beneficial vacation time alone. An extra day or two on the weekend costs little.

Transportation normally costs less if you stay over Saturday night. In major cities where hotels are crowded during the week with business people, hotels often offer specially reduced rates during the weekend. The extra day or two of vacation gives you time for quality thinking and reinforces your confidence in being able to enjoy being by yourself from time to time. Before we move on to the last GEM relationship, take some time to focus on whatever thoughts or feelings have surfaced as you journeyed through Intimacy and Solitude.

Look back at your notes and examine the questions you answered. Try to let new information about yourself come into your awareness. Whatever you do, don't judge this new information or make a determination that you must do something with it, just take the information in and let it be there with you. Soon enough you will come to understand how new information can create positive change in your life.

As we leave Intimacy and Solitude, remind yourself that you are capable of great depth and commitment in your life. You have the right to share your joy and your sadness with people who care about you and respect who you are. You possess great internal resources. Your mind is capable of great achievement.

It is my hope that the GEM model is helping you to realize your uniqueness and personal value, but don't expect all of the answers to appear right away. Just know that there are always options and always choices, when you have the courage to confront change for the purpose of growth.

Chapter Eleven

Equality/Manipulation Relationship: Issues

~ ~

How you satisfy your need for Equality and Manipulation can dramatically affect your behavior and how you deal with people. In this chapter, you will learn more about the significance of these two needs, their influence and impact on your life. If you want more respect and self-empowerment, you need to act out of these two needs with greater awareness and sensitivity. Although the words Equality and Manipulation are familiar to you, test your knowledge by answering these questions:

1. Have I ever thought about how I meet these needs within myself?
2. Do I understand what positive outcomes can be obtained when I create balance between my needs for Equality and Manipulation?
3. Am I aware of the connection between these two needs and my Self-Love and Self-Power needs?
4. Do I understand how Equality and Manipulation are demonstrated through my behavior?

~ ~

If you didn't answer yes to all four questions, what you will discover in this chapter should be very helpful.

Fulfilling and balancing your Equality and Manipulation needs help you erase the negative biases and prejudices you learned growing up. Erasing them is crucial if you want to deal effectively with how men and women experience their worlds differently. It also will help you to establish more successful personal and professional relationships.

In our society, the word Equality has a more positive connotation than Manipulation. But as freely as the powerful word Equality is used, many people don't understand its deeper meaning and purpose.

Unfortunately, they overlook their internal need for Equality because they don't recognize its inspirational and motivational value. They tend to think of this word only in its social or political context.

In contrast, Manipulation is not a word readily used. Most folks have a negative feeling about this word. This is especially true of women. Manipulation is one of the more misunderstood and misinterpreted gender-sensitive words in our society. By proper definition, it simply implies skill. But interestingly, while it is considered shrewd for men to master this skill as a way to ensure success, women who master this skill are often thought of (by both women and men) as being deceptive, unethical or conniving.

Women and men alike need to understand that when this need is adequately met and balanced it can only be positive. Both genders need to master this practical skill to succeed. They also need to acknowledge that Manipulation can be misused or abused by either sex. As long as you misinterpret its purpose and define Manipulation differently for each gender, your belief in Equality for yourself and others will suffer. Positive Manipulation increases the level of Equality you experience.

Creating balance between this pair of needs increases your belief in your own ability. When you acknowledge and meet your needs for Equality and Manipulation, you create a lifestyle that encompasses independence, flexibility and creativity. As with all of your needs, you are responsible for fulfilling these two.

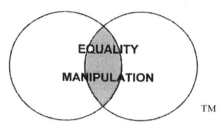

Here, again, are the definitions for Equality and Manipulation.

Equality: the conviction that you are unique, that your contribution in life is valuable to yourself and to others and that you and all people are of equal value as human beings.

Manipulation: the ability to exercise Self-Power to create positive change, to influence and control your personal environment; it is the intuitive quality of knowing your needs and those of others and working to meet those needs.

Remember, these two GEM needs are the least obvious to recognize as internal needs. Often they're thought of as external and distant from our internal need system. Familiarize yourself with these definitions so you can become more aware of their importance.

~ ~

The Equality Need

The need for Equality exists in each of us. If you don't believe you're entitled to a purposeful, enjoyable, rewarding life, your internal need for Equality is not being met.

Your desire for Equality and your ability to meet this need depend on your understanding of it. Fulfillment of this need enhances your self-image and self-value. But unless you believe Equality has something worthwhile to offer, your interest in fulfilling it may go unnoticed.

Most of us don't realize the relevance of this subtle need. Wonderful benefits can be derived from Equality. One is the realization that you're not threatened or intimidated by someone else's personality or talents.

How many times have you felt intimidated by another person? Few of us can deny having felt such a feeling. It's not unusual to be intimidated by someone who has some quality you perceive yourself as lacking. But if you've met your need for Self-Love, Self-Power, Intimacy and Solitude and you acknowledge Equality as another internal need that must be satisfied, someone else's strengths and talents no longer threaten you.

Choosing to live with Equality in your life increases your ability to see alternatives and solutions. When your need for Equality is satisfied, you become more self-assured and comfortable making decisions. When your Equality need is not met, your thinking becomes restrictive and motivates you inappropriately. Acquiring an internal sense of this need will show you that your options in life are limitless, giving you the energy to exercise your unlimited potential and increase your level of internal comfort.

~ ~

Family History

During your childhood, it is likely that whatever information you received about Equality pertained to your external world rather than to your internal world. The external way of thinking about Equality explains why so many people neglect this internal need. Discussions about Equality were probably rare among the adults in your life, and few of you had the good fortune to grasp its more personal meaning. If you didn't see Equality modeled through the behavior of these influential adults, you had even less reason to challenge its meaning and purpose to you.

If you did witness Equality through someone's behavior, it may not have been explained to you as a positive internal need. Without such discussion, perhaps you came to a conclusion that Equality simply meant to act in a fair way. Or maybe you thought of Equality as it applies to gender, cultural or racial issues. Whatever you thought then, we hope you now know that Equality means much more.

Do You Need Equality?

Equality speaks from that place deep within where your opinion of yourself continues to grow. When you believe in your own Equality, you reflect this belief through your behavior and through developing a belief system that allows you to manage your life equitably and out of self-respect.

You minimize your weaknesses and maximize your strengths when you create more Equality in your life. Don't be fooled by the fact that Equality isn't a basic survival need such as water, food or shelter. It's a powerful resource that you can use to realize potential, success and inner peace.

Equality is part of your internal map. When you follow it, your outside world is less stressful and, internally, you are more content.

When you are fair-minded, you'll make less unrealistic demands of yourself and others. Learn to appreciate this need and build upon it. Learn to understand how Equality fits with the other GEM needs. This knowledge is a big step toward living more effectively.

Equality vs. Selfishness

Equality is often confused with selfishness. Many people believe that if they demand and expect Equality for themselves, they are being selfish. If you believe this, take the time now to answer the four questions below. Pay close attention to your reactions. If you feel any discomfort, doubt, confusion or agitation, you may be holding yourself back in some way. When it comes to yourself, you may not know what is and what isn't fair. You may not know how to satisfy your need for Equality or how to command the respect you deserve.

1. Are you content with the amount of respect you command?
2. Do you respect other people and encourage them in their endeavors? List at least three people outside of your family whom you have helped to get ahead.
3. Can you join with other women and men on their level and appreciate them for who they are and where they are?
4. Do you believe that you are effective?

If you answered all four questions with a "yes," give yourself credit for being an inquisitive, adventurous, evolving person. Keep doing whatever you're doing — obviously, you're doing something right! But keep learning so you can continue to evolve. That's one of the secrets to success.

Women, in general, seem to have more difficulty meeting their need for Equality than men do, but men often misinterpret this need as well. Reread my definition of Equality to remind you of the importance of valuing yourself and of treating your uniqueness as you would treat someone else's. The truth is, selfish people don't value themselves! You can only give away what you have, so loving yourself is where it all begins. This is what Equality is all about.

A Woman Who Was Confused

Shirley was a woman whose Self-Love and Self-Power needs were well-balanced. She enjoyed Intimacy with herself and with others, but was not quite as comfortable with Solitude. All of us have room for improvement, and Shirley was no exception. This fifty-one-year-old woman came into counseling because she was unsure about her future. Although she was pleased with most of the choices she had made throughout her life, she couldn't shake her restless and sometimes empty feeling. Living in a depressed state was not acceptable to Shirley. So for this questioning woman, the next logical step was to find some answers.

"I believe this is a perfect time in my life to seek some outside help," she told me. "I have no regrets that I chose to be a full-time homemaker and mother. I never felt compro-

~ ~

mised in any way. I was doing what I wanted to do, but my life today is a different story. My three children are independent and on their own, and my husband, now that he is semi-retired, is enjoying his hobbies. I have gone from never having had enough time to having too many hours in a day. Volunteering fills some of these hours but it doesn't make me feel productive enough. I've never been much for organizational projects, so I can only do a certain amount of these types of things before I feel bored. I feel I haven't any important purpose anymore. I watch my husband reap the rewards of his hard work, and my children are eager to pursue their careers. Even my youngest, who's still in college, is having the time of his life, and here I am with nothing to look forward to. In some ways, I resent all of them, and that makes me feel guilty."

As Shirley continued to talk, it became apparent that her need for Equality was not being met adequately. Shirley scored low on the Solitude portion of the test, so it's not surprising that this energetic woman also felt confused about her personal interests. She had not spent any worthwhile time thinking about them.

Shirley is a classic example of how the GEM needs build on one another. When one GEM need isn't satisfied, the other internal needs are impaired. Her lack of Solitude fulfillment made it difficult for Shirley to create balance between her Solitude and Intimacy needs. This, in turn, made it hard for her to achieve balance in meeting her Equality and Manipulation needs. It takes more than satisfying one or two internal needs to complete a self picture that feels right and whole. Visualize yourself as *you* would like to be. Then get busy meeting the internal need or needs that will let your picture become a reality. In the process, remember that Equality, as subtle as it is, is an important piece of your internal puzzle. It enables you to move in and out of your daily involvements and activities with greater self-assurance and purpose.

Here is what Shirley was missing. Everything she supported and encouraged in the lives of her husband and children she had forgotten to encourage in herself. Her internalized belief was that one should value oneself enough to seek a life of meaning and purpose, but she had neglected to apply this belief to herself. It generally takes a major change before a person challenges her or his internal need for Equality. In Shirley's effort to be a "good" wife and mother, she ignored her own needs and personal interests. She had invested herself in her husband and her children and the cost was that she had buried her own purpose.

Shirley's family history taught her the importance of the other GEM needs, and this was apparent in her overall positive attitude and outlook. But she still bought into a generational message that a woman's rewards and gratifications come from "giving to" and "developing" loved ones. A family philosophy such as this does not cultivate the thought that it's equally important to be thoughtful and concerned with your own talent and purpose. Instead, this message often is misinterpreted to mean that any self-purpose is selfish.

Biases and Prejudices Attached to Equality

Your journey through the GEM needs encourages you to think about your internal map. I have repeatedly stressed the importance of challenging that place within you that stores all of your emotions. Take this time to reread the Family History section of this chapter. Think about your own family and how Equality was played out within your

~ ~

household. If you were raised in an orphanage or in foster homes, how was Equality presented in these unique environments? What messages did you receive about Equality while you were growing up?

I interviewed many women and men, asking each, "How would you define Equality?" As you read their answers, think about the following questions:
1.   Would you answer this question the same way?
2.   How else might you define Equality?
3.   Do you agree with most of the statements?
4.   Can you distinguish which answers represented messages from the speaker's childhood?

Below are some of the answers I received from people I interviewed and to whom I posed the question, "How would you define Equality?"

"I believe in myself, so I value my opinion."

"My father was a fair man; he looked at all sides of an issue and he always listened to everyone's point of view. I guess to me Equality means that type of fairness."

"Things were never fair in our house. No one respected anything of anyone else's. It didn't matter what it was. Nothing was sacred. I never thought about Equality because we didn't have it."

"I remember when the schools began to integrate; this was the first time that I can remember ever hearing the word Equality."

"My mother was a feminist, so I was brought up on the word 'Equality.' I think it was the most important word in our house. I believe in it."

"Without it, our country wouldn't be what it is."

"Women in the workplace still suffer from a lack of it."

"They never taught me about Equality in school. Isn't

that the most logical place to learn about Equality?"

"It's the desire to treat others in a fair way. You learn this from your parents."

"Our society works at it, and probably does better than most, but we aren't even close to living in a society that respects the rights of all humans, and that to me is what Equality is all about."

Many of these women and men said they were never formally taught about Equality. Most felt they learned about Equality by living within a society and learning how to get along with others. A few believed that Equality was not something you choose to possess, but that you earn through power, success, money or status. The majority did not think about Equality as an internal need, nor did they recognize it as something that contributed to their effectiveness.

In our society, as in many societies and cultures, Equality is more readily acquired and achieved by men because men have been more valued than women. This bias teaches that women are not equal to men, so women are forced to work twice as hard as men to prove themselves. This has created unreasonable hardships for women.

The notion that in some way men are better than women has been substantiated and supported not only by society, but by the people who continually keep this ridiculous belief alive — from the political system, where men have always been considered the authority and held the greatest power, to the religious system, which (with some recent exceptions) has been a man's domain. Even today, the workplace continues to devalue the worth of women by paying them lower wages than men. No doubt, our family system does the worst damage. It still delivers messages in our earliest teachings that imply that women are caretakers and nurturers, not decision or policy-makers. Together, all

~ ~

of these systems perpetuate an inequitable gender bias.

As long as women are not taught positive, healthy ways to empower themselves, they will continue to devalue themselves and to diminish their right to Equality. They will not meet the challenge to fulfill this need. As a result, women will continue to expect less than they deserve and accept gender bias. If this passive acceptance prevails, men will not be forced to re-examine their own definitions and beliefs about Equality.

The bias that men are more valuable than women devalues men as well, but in a more subtle way. It creates for men a false sense of their rights and their power. Men's perspective of Equality tends to be similar to their view of fair play in a sporting event. There's a winner and a loser — anything in between is just part of the game! With this outlook, men are robbed of their deeper emotions, which could give them richer insight. This is a huge loss for men because our deeper emotions allow us to call on and use our intuition when the facts aren't adding up.

Because society emphasizes outside power and man's quest to achieve it, most men have not experienced authentic Equality. So its advantages remain foreign to them. Even today, in spite of our dramatic growth and drastic changes, most religious and ethnic groups as well as a large part of our society continue to place men in a superior position, requiring women to remain reverent. This philosophy indirectly supports inequity between the genders by creating an imbalance of their relative positions. Under this system, there is no real push for men to look at this need differently or to confront how their own Equality needs are being compromised. Because men do have more Equality than women, they have not played a major part in creating change. Is there any wonder that today's workplace is filled with confusion, hostility, unhealthy competition and dissatisfied employees?

Without Equality, it's impossible to expect a peaceful and constructive environment. Today's relationships and today's families suffer dramatically because of this destructive bias. It places too much emphasis on a man's ability to succeed and too little emphasis on a woman's right to succeed.

The Manipulation Need

The word Manipulation generally creates a negative picture. For a few moments, clear your head of any interpretations you have of Manipulation. I want you to think of this word as a strategy you are learning about for the first time.

Let's review the definition of Manipulation: the ability to exercise Self-Power to create positive change, to influence and control your environment, it is the intuitive quality of knowing your needs and those of others and working to meet those needs.

Below are eight descriptions of Manipulation, all of which are positive. As you read each, notice your first reactions. Just for fun, get together with a few friends or family members and experiment with them using this exercise. Ask each of them to share their first reactions to each of the following statements. Don't be surprised at what discussions transpire.

1. Manipulation is positive.
2. Manipulation is a learned skill.
3. Manipulation is exciting.
4. Manipulation is an application.
5. Manipulation is an internal need.

~ ~

   6. Manipulation is control.

   7. Manipulation is powerful.

   8. Manipulation is creative.

Given that these descriptions are accurate, it is easy to understand why meeting this need is valuable to you. Can you think of any reason you wouldn't want to possess the positive qualities of flexibility and control that Manipulation provides?

To Manipulate in ways that are positive and purposeful, you must fulfill and balance it with Equality, with good conscious intentions motivating your behavior. You should never manipulate from a hidden agenda.

Family History

Manipulation is a learned skill. Reaching back into your family history to explore how the adults in your life manipulated will shed light on how you view Manipulation today. Here is an activity that will help you do this:

Record your answers and keep them for future reference. You may want to keep this list indefinitely so you can compare your previous Manipulation skills with your future beliefs and behavior. Answer each question with the first answer that pops into your head.

Try not to take too much time thinking about it. If you can't answer a question, leave it and go on. So take some Solitary time to turn inward to your Intimate Self to seek your answers.

   1. Do you remember how the adults in your life Manipulated?

   2. In your family, who used Manipulation in a negative way? Who used it in a positive way? How did they do this?

3. Were you taught to Manipulate?
4. Did you respect the person who taught you?
5. In your family, did one Manipulate for the sake of accomplishment?
6. If one Manipulated for something other than accomplishment, list the other purposes.
7. Name one type of positive Manipulation.
8. Name one type of negative Manipulation.
9. Do you think men Manipulate more than women?
10. Do you believe that you Manipulate every day?
11. Can Manipulation be an asset in your professional world?
12. Is it necessary to Manipulate in order to teach?
13. Is it the intention behind the behavior that determines whether the Manipulation is positive or negative?
14. Can a person be effective without Manipulating?
15. When you were growing up, did you learn about Manipulation in a positive way?
16. Do you know when you are Manipulating?
17. Do you know when you are being Manipulated?
18. Are you conscious of how you Manipulate?

This activity offers a lot of hidden information about yourself. Remember, sometimes out of fear, you may avoid new information about yourself, or perhaps you're unsure as to how you'll handle the new information. Somewhere in the back of your mind, you know that most information about yourself is not new; it is old information waiting to be remembered, and its recollection may cause you emotional discomfort.

But a benefit of satisfying your Manipulation need is using your power to manipulate your thoughts and feelings

~ ~

at your own pace. Going at your own pace is the only way to ensure control over your own emotional comfort while learning.

Each member in every family has a unique style of manipulating. If you think about how the adults in your childhood accomplished their goals and made their world work for them, you may see how their actions and beliefs spilled over into you. This will be especially true if you're trying to remember how they influenced you and other people.

A Man Who Was Deceitful

Allen and Elaine came to marriage counseling after Elaine threatened a divorce. Elaine had noticed that Allen was increasingly aloof and moody. "He picks fights for no reason, and he hasn't bought me a present for any occasion in over two years. It seems the more I work to cover the expenses, the more he bets larger sums of money playing golf and playing cards."

Allen quickly jumped in to defend himself. "I don't play for big money. Besides, I'm always ahead. That's what she's really angry about — it's not our marriage."

"I'm so glad he said that," Elaine countered, "because I can't seem to make him understand that it's not the hobbies that bother me, it's much more. I don't feel we're partners, and I don't feel he cares about how hard I work. Money has been very tight for us and I've been the main source of our income.

"At first, I thought he was just having some bad business breaks. Then I began to realize that he always finds fault with his bosses and eventually quits his job. It's a pattern. I'm exhausted from the worry and the feeling that

I'm the only person who is looking out for our future."

After several therapy sessions, Elaine called for an emergency appointment. She came to the session alone, in terrible distress. That morning, she had found Allen's paycheck stub and discovered that he had been given a substantial raise. Elaine called the bookkeeper with a reasonable story and found out that the raise had taken place more than four months earlier. Her trust in Allen was shattered. "He never told me about this, and he hasn't contributed any more to our household, yet he claims he doesn't have any money, so where has it been going?" As she continued to cry, she kept uttering how betrayed she felt.

Elaine had been betrayed. She had been lied to and deceived. In the end, it was uncovered that Allen was gambling heavily. He was not concerned about his wife in a way that was sensitive or caring, and he didn't worry about their financial situation. When confronted, Allen simply shrugged his shoulders and said, "She worries too much. What can creditors do to us anyway?"

Allen's life goals and his concept of a relationship were quite different from Elaine's. But he wasn't honest enough with himself to examine his lack of maturity concerning his responsibilities to the relationship. Instead, he negatively manipulated his environment to get only his needs met. Many people start out this way, but sometime during their adult life they learn to become more mature and sensitive to the needs of others.

When you understand and respect the difference between positive Manipulation and negative Manipulation, you will be aware of how this powerful strategy affects other people. Because Allen had not met and balanced his own internal needs in a healthy way, he was unable to

~ ~

consider Elaine's needs. It was somewhat predictable that his need for Manipulation would be misdirected and out of balance. Allen left Elaine and, in less than a month, was living with someone else, still not understanding why his marriage to Elaine had failed. His lack of insight and his resistance to change kept him on a misdirected path.

Unfortunately, he had never satisfied his need for Self-Love and Self-Power. His Intimacy and Solitude needs suffered because of this deficiency, so it was predictable that he would manipulate in a negative self-serving way.

Like Allen, many people lack self-control. Without a feeling of control in your life, you can't negotiate personal success in a positive way. Manipulation is the skill that provides the flexibility to be creative. It encourages self-control because it enhances your feelings of Self-Power. With "healthy" power (Self-Power), the only manipulating you will choose to do will have a positive intent.

Have you ever noticed that the people you most admire generally control their lives and the world around them with a sense of calm? The type of calm we are talking about requires flexibility and is very noticeable. The women and men who enjoy this calm have positive Manipulation skills, and because of these skills, they stand out from other people. We'll explore the positive characteristics of these women and men in the next chapter.

Biases and Prejudices Attached to Manipulation

The most common gender bias attached to Manipulation suggests that women manipulate in negative ways to gain control, whereas men need to manipulate in order to control their environment. This biased view of how and why men and women manipulate supports the uneven distribution of power that women and men experience even today.

Most people have fixed ideas about how women and men are supposed to exercise influence over others. These ideas are built into fairly rigid gender-role expectations that prevent women from using the influence styles that are accepted for men. People react in a negative or positive way to how well others conform to their sex-role boundaries. When they behave "normally," they're rewarded; when they behave in a way that doesn't fit the sex-role stereotype, they're punished by being criticized or even ostracized. For example, aggression is not acceptable for a woman, and society frowns on any style that is seen as coercive or threatening. While the threat of punishment or the withholding of expected rewards may be effective, the woman who employs these techniques generally is disliked and avoided.

Women also are seen as less competent but more warm and emotional than men, and these stereotypes erect barriers that reduce women's chances of controlling their personal environment directly. Because it's appropriate for men to adopt a more aggressive, forceful Manipulation style, men tend to be more direct than women in getting others to do what they want. A young man who wants a raise in his allowance might approach his father with a direct request, perhaps pointing out a few facts that could help his case. A young woman who wants a raise in her allowance often follows a more indirect route. She might first confide in one of her parents about a personal matter and then hint about needing more money. Or she might smile and apologize some, taking a helpless rather than a competent approach. For some women, using adult power or Manipulation means a loss of feminine sensitivity and compassion. This loss presents a sense of conflict that can be disturbing.

Researchers have also found that women tend to use non-verbal Manipulation methods more than men. One woman I know leaves newspapers and magazine ads around the house when she wants a particular item as a birthday or Christmas gift. She's convinced that if she were to ask for it directly, her husband would be upset.

When women break away from these binding stereo-types and adopt a healthy, mature view of Manipulation, they still tend to look at power differently than men do. Women are more concerned than men with both sides of a relationship and are quicker to recognize their own interde-pendence. While men think of power and Manipulation as assertion and aggression, women see acts of nurturing as strength. In most home situations, women exercise Manipulation mostly to help nurture and take care of others in the family.

Power Sources at Work

Power to manipulate your work environment comes from several sources, including the position you hold, your ability to reward or punish subordinates and the amount of respect others have for you. But how much influence you have is generally determined by four factors: status, resources, expertise and confidence. Societal, cultural and gender biases limit women's ability to manipulate in the workplace. This carries through each of the four power factors:

Status. A high status increases your ability to manip-ulate others. People assume that if your status is high, you have all the other three power factors—resources, expertise, and confidence. At home, women have status through being a mother or a wife, but that status usually doesn't carry forward to the workplace. Status is obtained through wealth, education, or a high-level job. Unfortunately, women in the United States have less wealth, less education, and fewer top-level jobs than men. So women often have less status and, consequently, less opportunity to manipulate.

Resources. Men are in control of most resources in the U.S. The wealthiest individuals in America are mostly men. Even when women have resources, many people assume they're not able to control them. At work, the higher the managerial level, the more resources are controlled by the manager. As of 1990, less than 3% of the top-level managerial jobs in this nation were held by women. But women have made major inroads into low and mid-level managerial jobs. As women move up the managerial ranks, they will control more resources.

Expertise. Experts have special resources such as knowledge, information, or skills. The top authorities in most fields today are considered to be men because female experts have less exposure and power than their male counterparts. Many female experts have not been acknowledged as such.

Self-Confidence. Most people who have status, resources and expertise also have self-confidence and the confidence of others. Because women tend to have less status and fewer resources and are not acknowledged as experts, they tend to have less self-confidence than men, especially in the presence of men. People with low self-confidence have less power to manipulate their personal environment because other people don't respect them.

~ ~

Sex and Power

Sex can be used as a means of control. Men and women often confuse sex and power, both at home and at work. At work, this presents special problems and serious liabilities. Sexual harassment is one of the major problems that infects all aspects of a workplace.

The confusion surrounding sex and power presents a problem to both genders.

Historically, the workplace has been male-dominated, so men have not needed to monitor their behavior. With increasing numbers of women in today's workplace, men need to look at how they communicate with women. And women need to confront their past ways of getting recognition in the workplace.

Women must understand that when the focus of attention is shifted from a woman's professionalism or expertise to her appearance or to her sexuality, the woman loses power and authority. And men need to understand that they demean women when they turn their relationships with women from work colleague connections into male-female connections.

A Woman Who Knew How to Manipulate

Ceil knew Manipulation was a positive skill and her effective personality was living proof of her ability to manipulate in a positive way. She had been taught by her parents that she wouldn't succeed if she didn't accept the responsibility of manipulating her environment. Throughout our interview, Ceil gave me many examples of how the right intentions naturally lead to positive Manipulation. She stressed that her successful climb to the top had never

~ ~

required manipulating at the cost of anyone else. Rather, she told me, she had used opportunity after opportunity to help others while manipulating her own destiny.

Ceil's candid description of this misunderstood internal need was remarkably accurate. She said, "Although I never thought of Manipulation as being an internal need, I definitely knew it was important. Thanks to my parents, I understand how Manipulation works for me. I'm aware of its power and use this power with great respect.

"I believe the word Manipulation has been given too much negative attention. Let's face it, we all manipulate. I wouldn't hire a manager who didn't know how to manipulate in a positive way. It's a necessity."

Ceil was comfortable with Manipulation because of her parents' influence. They taught her that Manipulation was a skill. Ceil also independently nurtured her internal needs through thoughtful attention to them.

Like many successful, effective people, Ceil did not hesitate to use Manipulation to maximize her potential. It's critical to take the threat out of the word Manipulation and to become comfortable with this skill, which we use daily. Don't avoid calling it by its proper name. Manipulation deserves to be understood and fulfilled in a positive way.

Chapter Twelve

Equality/Manipulation Relationship: Characteristics

~ ~

Creating internal balance between Equality and Manipulation is a major step toward becoming more effective. Balance between these two needs is especially important when you need to be in charge, take control or accomplish a task.

As with all of the GEM needs, you can internally balance and fulfill these two needs only after you take full responsibility for all that you are and all that you are not. Gender biases and prejudices if still a part of your belief system will continue to inhibit your potential.

Any negative belief or thought is an enemy, ready to attack your desire to achieve. To combat this enemy, use what knowledge you've learned so far, and then stretch yourself even further for more information and guidance. As you have been doing throughout these self-reflective activities, use your determination to open up to new information. Accept these insights and trust yourself to choose only the information that is exactly right for you.

~ ~

Creating balance between your Equality and Manipulation needs is a completion of GEM'S internal map. This pair of needs and their relationship to one another are fascinating because Equality and Manipulation aren't as common as the other four GEM needs.

Equality and Manipulation each have distinctive characteristics. Their relationship to one another and the balance between them act as a pipeline to your outside world. How effectively you operate within this outside world is a direct result of how much internal balance you create.

Tell yourself to think about Equality and Manipulation without judging them as good or bad, negative or positive. If you can do this, your experience of these two needs will give you much more awareness. The greatest awareness is realizing that there is no such thing as positive Manipulation without Equality and vice versa.

Internal balance between Equality and Manipulation maintains and stabilizes your other internal needs. Once you accept that it takes a balanced rhythm flowing between all of these internal needs to achieve internal harmony (which produces positive goals), you will understand the importance of making this internal dance happen.

Here are some questions that, when answered, will help you to check how effective you are now.

1. Do I feel the amount of inner contentment and satisfaction that I want to feel in my present life?
2. Am I willing to reevaluate myself and my life in order to confront any present circumstance or situation that creates discontentment or unhappiness?
3. Do I believe I am the creator of my personal environment?
4. Do I feel of equal value to others?

5. Do I contribute to my world?
6. Do I enjoy my present work environment?
7. Do I enjoy my present personal environment?
8. Do I expect others to contribute to their own worlds?
9. Do I elicit the help of others?
10. Do I feel I earn the respect of others?
11. Do I treat others with respect?
12. Do I know what it takes to create a harmonious environment?

If you're not happy with your answers, you're not as effective as you could be. It's important to remember that "perfect" doesn't exist, but you can have inner peace and self-satisfaction. That is what internal balance is all about!

Another way to think about internal balance is to think about the tremendous balance it takes to experience a successful, fulfilling relationship with another person. It takes two people dancing to a similar rhythm to establish and sustain their relationship. Both must always be seeking to accommodate and appreciate one another. Each must accept that it is never the job of only one person to be responsible for the state of the relationship. It requires that both people have a vested interest in working toward a commitment of individual growth and relationship growth.

There is no such thing as relationship growth without individual growth. The ideal of any relationship lies in mutual respect and sensitivity to change. It also requires an ability to create enough internal balance to allow the rhythm of the relationship to flow in whatever direction is needed at any given time. Your need for Equality and Manipulation and how you create balance between them affects all of the relationships in your life.

~ ~

People Whose Equality/Manipulation Needs Are in Balance

People who create internal balance between their Equality and Manipulation needs appreciate feelings of self-confidence and self-control on a daily basis.

They look forward to the challenges in life and accept what they can't change. Their openness and sense of fairness are inviting and create good will in their environment.

Their involvement in people, community and career is well-balanced and gives them great satisfaction and pleasure.

- ***They are creative.***

Their thinking is not rigid. They are free to let their minds explore interesting aspects of their personalities. They enjoy the challenge of creativity because they are not afraid to abandon an idea or a thought when it doesn't work in a favorable way.

- ***They are flexible.***

Flexibility is a major key to success. It frees you from behavior or beliefs that keep you stuck or operating with tunnel vision. Flexible people enjoy life to its greatest extent. They are not locked into predesigned or predetermined ways.

- ***They are comfortable with change and welcome it.***
- ***They are good motivators.***

Their ability to motivate themselves and others is directly related to the fact that they are comfortable with Manipulation and use it to produce positive outcomes. They recognize what it will take to accomplish their goals.

- ***They are good leaders.***

They enjoy making decisions and appreciate their Self-Power. They are fair with themselves and others, and they like to help. They lead with authority but never without sensitivity.

- ***They are empowering.***

Their ability to empower others comes from their ability to empower themselves. They take the time to find the strengths of another person and build upon them.

- ***They are good team players.***

Because they are fair and believe in equal value and equal contribution, they're able to be part of a team. They enjoy camaraderie and take pleasure in collective thinking and combined efforts.

- ***They are involved.***

Their ability to enjoy their outside world comes from their lack of fear of rejection or failure.

- ***They are willing to volunteer or take on assignments.***

They have an interest in their environment and play a role in its development and maintenance.

It's easy to comprehend the good feelings a person experiences when she or he has developed such qualities. But individuals don't just happen onto these strengths, they must be willing to work to acquire and develop them. Somewhere within themselves, they know that personal success can't be achieved without building most of these characteristics. So they withstand temporary emotional pain in order to identify their internal obstacles as a way to obtain these wonderful traits.

Women and men who create balance between Equality and Manipulation believe they have a right to control their personal environment.

They accept that they are of equal value. Neither the Manipulation nor its purpose is offensive to these women and men because they understand its positive meaning and value.

People Whose Equality/Manipulation Needs Are out of Balance

Women and men who are out of balance between Equality and Manipulation often suffer from feelings of professional inadequacy and personal dissatisfaction. These feelings usually are generated by a fear of having too little control over their lives. These women and men try to compensate for this imbalance in many ways, but their behavior either is ineffective or is effective at the cost of other people.

On the surface, they may appear to have fulfilled their Self-Love and Intimacy needs, but on closer examination of their relationships, something different is often revealed. Because their own Self-Love need is low and unfulfilled they feel uncomfortable with Intimacy, and tend to choose needy and dependent partners who are also low in Self-Love and Self-Power. These partners usually need a person who they can take care of as a way for them to feel worthwhile. So both people get what they need from the other. One pays constant homage while the other attempts to build his or her personal worth by accepting it.

People low or misdirected in Equality and Manipulation often feel they are not equal to others, so they are less assertive in their workplaces. This is unfortunate because, in the workplace, they are expected to establish themselves as capable of getting what they need and want.

This lack of assertion can be acted out with behavior that is overtly aggressive and insensitive to others, or it can play itself out with inflexible and disempowering behaviors. These women and men either feel entitled to take what they want with little consideration or respect for those around them, or they don't feel entitled to anything. They may become depressed when their lives are not giving them what they want, or they may become relentless.

They frequently let others take the credit that they deserve, which may lead to bitterness and a tendency to withhold. The flip side of this may also be true — a person whose Equality and Manipulation needs are not met and balanced may take all of the credit and constantly brag about herself or himself. Whatever the behavior, it's unappealing and inappropriate.

People Whose Equality Fulfillment Is Low or Misdirected

- *They experience feelings of inadequacy.*

They generally cover up these feelings with behavior that is critical, insensitive or judgmental.

- *They do not perceive themselves as valuable.*

They tend to undervalue themselves and either overvalue or devalue others.

- *They place responsibility onto others.*

They limit their amount of responsibility to avoid being wrong or feeling inadequate. This lack of action on their part creates even greater feelings of inadequacy.

- *They lack a sense of commitment.*

This keeps them from becoming too involved. They are often aloof, distant or mildly depressed.

~ ~

- *They are afraid to look at new things.*

Because they don't perceive their own value or the value of new things, they don't test their potential or experience new and exciting things. They remain trapped in the old, even when it's no longer satisfying.

- *They're critical of others or unfair in their judgment.*

Their own lack of contribution often is covered up by criticizing others.

- *They do not challenge their potential.*

Because they do not acknowledge the value of their contribution, they don't challenge enough of their potential.

A Man Whose Equality Fulfillment Was Low and Misdirected

Tim was a lawyer who had an exceptional talent for recognizing good business opportunities. Within his law firm, this expertise should have made him powerful and self-confident. But in the past ten years, his position in the firm had not advanced. At age forty-seven, he felt his professional life held little excitement or challenge.

Tim's wife was concerned as she watched him sink deeper into depression. Tim didn't appear to have any insight into or explanation for how he was feeling. He sloughed it off and made excuses.

Finally, Tim agreed to enter therapy, although he wasn't hopeful about the process. "I can't change anything, and I don't see anything better in my future," he confided. "I work hard but never really get ahead. I make twenty-five percent less than anyone else with my seniority, and I feel the firm is wasting my abilities. I'm loyal in spite of these inequities, and I remain committed; but I no longer feel enthusiastic or eager."

Tim's depression was only a symptom of his low and misdirected need for Equality. As Tim worked toward fulfilling this internal need the depression began to subside. This made it easier for him to concentrate on what he needed to do to change his situation. He began to question his lack of responsibility to himself and how this diminished his self-value. Although he was a fair-minded man, Tim failed to be fair with himself. He didn't confront or challenge his reluctance to contribute, nor did he present a picture of himself that commanded respect. Instead, he kept his talents and ideas to himself and devalued his contribution to the firm.

To address and resolve his issues surrounding his need for Equality, Tim began to explore the messages of his past. In doing this, he discovered where some of his emotional blocks were and how they were holding him back from getting what he wanted. As he became more assertive, he became more involved.

His biggest challenge occurred when he took the responsibility to generate new clients. Finally, Tim decided to act on a new belief about himself, that his ideas would be appreciated and welcomed.

Until this point, he had never acknowledged himself as someone who was as talented as his colleagues. After a few months, Tim took an assertive stand and asked for a raise. To his surprise, he was given the raise without question.

"I now understand how I needed to take more responsibility for what I needed to feel about myself. I knew I had a great talent for certain areas of business, but I never knew if anyone else could see that fact. I was too afraid to go out on a limb to prove myself."

What Tim was lacking was a belief in himself as a person of equal value, whose contributions were equally valuable. Without this belief, it was impossible for him to let his partners see or appreciate the talents that were unique to him.

None of us can present to the outside world the unique abilities that set us apart from others unless we accept the responsibility to believe it ourselves. We first must accept our contributions without comparing them to anyone else's.

If you have been reared in a family that weighed, measured and judged your every effort or ignored your efforts altogether, you may have decided that you were not a valuable person. As an adult and master of your destiny, it's crucial for you to reevaluate who you are and establish what you want to be.

People Whose Manipulation Fulfillment Is Low or Misdirected

- *They are not good team players.*

They have unrealistic expectations of others and often feel best only when they are in charge or in a superior position.
- *They are forceful in getting what they want.*

They are not concerned with the ways in which they get it. Their own needs and wants usually take priority over everyone else's.
- *They use people to their own advantage.*

They are not considerate or respectful of others. They see other people as objects to be used in their own efforts to get ahead.

- *They lack a sense of commitment.*

Their commitment is only to themselves. Their lack of commitment to others keeps them removed and often disrespectful.

- *They create discord in their environment.*

Due to their inability to appreciate others, they often interact negatively and create hostile environments.

- *They need to be controlling.*

Due to their feelings of insecurity and fear of loss of control, they need to control others as well as their environment. To them, control represents success, power and safety. Their controlling behavior is often hidden under the guise of being helpful.

- *They are suspicious of others' intentions.*

Because of their own ulterior motives, they suspect others of having hidden agendas also.

A Woman Whose Manipulation Fulfillment Was Low or Misdirected

Grace came into therapy after her supervisor demoted her from a management position. She was angry and confused about this decision. Grace's sister suggested that she seek therapy to examine the possibilities of why it happened.

This was the second time Grace had been removed from a managerial position. The first company told Grace that she was ineffective. Grace rationalized this away by blaming it on her boss, convinced that he was sexist and didn't like her. But when this second demotion was initiated by a woman supervisor who gave her a similar explanation, Grace was forced to question her earlier conclusion.

"My sister has been after me for years to get some counseling. She has always felt that I avoided getting close to people. She believes that my abruptness, as she calls it, is the reason for these demotions. I guess I'm not sure anymore what is going on, and I feel compelled to find out why this keeps happening. Obviously, something isn't right, and I'm very unhappy with where my professional life is *not* going."

After a brief update and some family history, Grace explored her internal needs and began to determine which needs were out of balance and unfulfilled in her life. It was difficult for her to look at her own behavior and take full responsibility for her actions and reactions. "It's painful to look at some of these things. I want things to be different, but I'm not convinced that therapy is the answer," she said.

With her sister's encouragement, Grace held on a little longer. She began to discover that much of her behavior was childlike and lacked sensitivity to other people and their problems. Her ability to manipulate people in positive ways was non-existent. In her attempt to meet her internal needs, she acted inappropriately. She did not really hear the complaints and ideas of those she supervised. She often ignored some of the men and women because she was unsure how to approach them. Due to her own insecurities, Grace presented herself as a distant, uncaring and uninvolved manager.

As the months went by, Grace learned to identify her misperception of the Manipulation need and how she wasn't satisfying it. She worked toward developing more favorable ways to motivate people. She took advantage of learning about positive ways to manipulate her environment, her behavior and her thinking. Without an awareness of her own need for internal balance, Grace had manipulated in a negative way. Like everyone else, Grace manipulated every day of her life, but she never acknowledged that fact.

"I always thought of Manipulation as something awful. Even the word sounded ugly to me. Now I realize that I do manipulate, and it's important for me to develop a good feeling about this skill in order to use it correctly. I also needed to be more aware of when and how I manipulate."

Grace remained in therapy until she felt comfortable with her new behavior change. She worked hard to develop her communication skills — skills that were sensitive and yet effective. She was proud of her efforts and pleased with the results.

Any type of personal change creates new self-awareness. As you undertake the solution-making process or work to adapt to change, you can't avoid your need to manipulate. Be grateful for these opportunities because they allow you to acknowledge how much a part of your life Manipulation is. Once you can acknowledge this, you can give yourself permission to deal with this skill positively and constructively.

Meeting your need for Equality and Manipulation and creating a healthy balance between them is the final step in your journey toward effectiveness. This step shouldn't be ignored any more than the steps you took to create balance between your other internal needs — especially if you seek to create a life filled with Self-Love, Self-Power, Intimacy, Solitude, Equality and Manipulation. These six GEM needs are vital to your total picture. Each of them designs a piece of your internal map and dictates your personal style of communication.

Don't avoid this final part of your internal journey. It's all part of your total self.

Before moving on, try to re-examine your need for Equality and Manipulation. Envision new ideas that you might like to try out or new feelings that you may want to experience.

Take one last look at the definitions for Equality and Manipulation and stretch yourself to incorporate these new definitions into your thinking. Play with the word Manipulation until you are comfortable with it. But don't water it down by replacing it with another word such as influence. Learn to be comfortable calling this skill by its proper name.

Now it's time to move on to the key action steps. You've come a long way, so it's reasonable to expect some changes—changes that will be positive and exciting once you become accustomed to them. Never forget that you have a vast ability to change.

Chapter Thirteen

Equality/Manipulation Relationship: Key Action Steps

~ ~

Before you journey into the key action steps, it will be helpful if you take some time to summarize what you explored in Chapters Eleven and Twelve. Think about your childhood again. Ask yourself, "What did I learn about my Equality and Manipulation needs?" Don't get hung up on the words themselves, just try to remember what you learned about these two needs.

As an example, while growing up, were you taught to be aware of your need for Equality and Manipulation? Or did you come to this on your own by watching and listening to others?

After spending a few minutes thinking back into your history, incorporate this information into your present life and compare it with your knowledge today. Think about what specific behaviors you have used to fulfill your need for Equality and Manipulation. Have those behaviors changed? Use the following activity to help this information surface and to help you gain additional insight.

Activity Instructions: Take a few minutes to relax and let your thoughts flow freely. Try not to focus on any one thing. Avoid any thoughts or feelings that represent problems or areas of concern. Remember to take some deep breaths through your nose, hold your breath for the count of four, then slowly exhale through your mouth. Do you feel relaxed? Begin by asking yourself about your childhood.

1. When I was growing up did I enjoy competitive games?
2. How did I feel when I won? How did I feel when I lost?
3. Did I make friends easily?
4. Did I have many friends or only one or two?
5. Was I able to influence people and win them over?
6. Did I like to contribute to classroom discussions?
7. Was I involved in team sports or organizations?
8. At what age did I start to take responsibility for myself?

The remainder of the questions have to do with the present:

9. Is my intuition good and do I trust it?
10. Do I like positions of power and independence?
11. Do people know where they stand with me?
12. Do I expect to meet my needs?
13. Are my expectations for myself and others reasonable?
14. If I am asked what I would like to make for a salary am I able to state what I feel I'm worth or do I ask for less?
15. How do I know that I am of value? How do I let other people know my value?

16. Do I recognize the value of others? How do I acknowledge this?
17. After reading Chapters Eleven and Twelve, did I feel more comfortable with my need for Manipulation?
18. Does my behavior demonstrate and demand Equality?
19. Did I learn anything new about Equality?
20. Do I need to change anything about how I Manipulate?

Don't look for a right or wrong answer. There are none. This is simply a way to surface some of your old information, giving yourself the chance to compare it with new insight.

If you found these questions easy to answer and you felt comfortable with your answers, chances are good that you grew up with an awareness of these two internal needs and believed they were important to your life.

But if you found yourself dissatisfied with your answers or hesitant while answering, it's probably fair to assume that your Equality and Manipulation needs are not as much in balance as they need to be. So give more attention to these two internal needs and create more balance between them.

It is hoped that Chapters Eleven and Twelve helped you understand Equality and Manipulation as they relate to your present life and to your overall effectiveness. The key action steps in this chapter will increase the communication skills that lead to your effectiveness. These steps will be of benefit to you if you want to gain a broader perspective of the world and the people in it. Remember, each person is different, so your methods of communication need to be flexible.

~ ~

As an internal map that directs you to each internal need, the GEM model reminds you that each of these internal needs is consciously or unconsciously trying to find fulfillment and balance. This affects your behavior.

It's important not to lose sight of this fact; the quality of your effectiveness depends on your behavior. The way you communicate, present yourself and act in general is directly tied to your internal need system.

Discovering how you operate out of these six internal needs will tell you more about yourself and others than any other way of learning.

Equality is the need that addresses your value as a human being. Operating with a healthy amount of self-value is the only way to feel comfortable about expecting and accepting the success that you have worked to attain. It's the need that allows you to give yourself credit whenever you are deserving.

Equality also helps you appreciate others and enjoy giving them whatever credit they deserve. This need helps build such positive qualities as honesty, loyalty and integrity.

Manipulation is the need that speaks to your intuitiveness, that special ability that taps into a deeper comprehension of whatever issues you are dealing with. This need allows you the freedom to enjoy change.

Manipulation gives you just the right amount of control over your life and allows you to be productive, powerful, and effective.

When your behavior demonstrates that you understand the purpose of balancing these two needs, you will have the tools to make your environment more pleasing.

Key Action Steps

How to Satisfy Your Need for Equality in Your Personal Life:

- **Step 1. Believe in Yourself.**

  You are a valuable person. Know this and act in ways that acknowledge and respect this fact. Here are some examples of simple but positive behaviors that say, "you are valuable." Use these behaviors and create others.
  - Make good eye contact when you speak.
  - Speak in an audible tone of voice.
  - Speak with confidence and assurance.
  - Try new things without fearing failure.
  - Involve yourself with other people and try new projects.
  - Experiment with your hidden talents, stretching your potential.
- **Step 2. Treat yourself fairly.**

  When you're too hard on yourself you diminish and devalue your personal equality. People who treat themselves fairly expect good things to happen. They create opportunities for themselves because they believe they deserve to have these opportunities.

  At the end of each day for seven days, ask yourself if you have treated yourself fairly. Take the time to think about your day, then ask yourself, "Did anything happen today that made me feel uncomfortable, angry, depressed or upset?" If the answer is "yes," think about that situation and try to come up with a different way you could have acted or reacted, a way that would have been more fair to you. If your answer was "no," move on and give yourself credit for achieving a satisfying day.

~ ~

- ***Step 3. Treat others fairly.***

You must treat others fairly if you want to experience yourself and your relationships in a meaningful way. Even more important to your total effectiveness is your desire to treat people fairly because you appreciate and respect who they are as individuals.

Using the same activity as in Step 2 (above), rethink your day and ask the same questions as they apply to others.

- ***Step 4. Don't compare yourself to others.***

Whenever you find that you are comparing yourself to another person, make a conscious decision to stop that type of thinking. Replace those thoughts by thinking about something that you appreciate about yourself. Start each morning with a good thought about yourself, and see if you can add more good thoughts to your list.

- ***Step 5. Accept your faults and weaknesses.***

If you can't accept that you have faults and weaknesses, you won't be able to experience self-acceptance. Everyone has faults and weaknesses. It's normal, so embrace them and get into the challenge of correcting them.

- ***Step 6. Have fun with yourself.***

People who know how to have fun with themselves feel more entitled to the good things in life. Answer the following questions to find out whether you know how to have fun with yourself.

1. Do you like to laugh?
2. Are you able to laugh at yourself?
3. Do you find enjoyable activities to do alone?
4. Do you enjoy the company of other people, and do you plan fun things with others?
5. Do you enjoy light comedy in the forms of books, plays, television programs, or movies?
6. Do you believe you are entertaining to others?

7. Do you like to be entertained by others?
8. Do you share fun stories with others?
9. Are you able to find humor in most day-to-day events?
10. On occasion, are you able to laugh until you cry? When was the last time you did that?

If you cannot answer each of these questions with a definite "yes," you need to work on this aspect of your personality. Lighten up. Try to be around happy people. Find fun things to do. Knowing how to have fun is critical to meeting your need for Equality.

- ***Step 7. Know that every situation has alternatives.***

When you meet your need for Equality, you can recognize that alternatives are always available. You are never trapped. Enjoy the freedom of this knowledge and don't hesitate to act on it. Every time you look for a solution or face a dilemma with the intent to correct it, you are acting on this knowledge.

- ***Step 8. Keep yourself well-informed.***

Keep up with day-to-day world events. This will keep you informed, involved and more interesting as a person. Try to subscribe to a daily newspaper and at least one entertaining magazine. Listen to the news at least once a day. Speak to others about what you read.

- ***Step 9. Be conscious of your biases and prejudices.***

Accept that you have biases and prejudices. Only with this awareness will you become sensitive to others. To meet your personal need for Equality, it is crucial to develop a sensitivity to others. This can only be accomplished through personal awareness.

~ ~

- *Step 10. Incorporate personal equality affirmations into your daily routine.*

Memorize the following statements. Once you memorize them, make a conscious effort to repeat them aloud to yourself at least three times a day: in the morning, during your work day and in the evening before going to bed.

- – I am a person of value.
- – I like to have fun with myself.
- – I like to learn new things about myself.
- – I am entitled to a good life.
- – I have my own resources.

How to Satisfy Your Need for Equality in Your Work Life:

- *Step 1. Understand the value of others.*

When you believe others have value, you treat them with more respect, more fairness. To be effective, you must know how to find value in another person. To do this, you need to be able to:

- – See another person for who she or he really is.
- – Hear what another person is really saying.
- – Feel what another person is really experiencing.
- – Treat others as you would want to be treated and as they want to be treated.

- *Step 2. Be friendly to co-workers.*

When you are friendly, you encourage good feelings and establish good rapport. Equality in the workplace cannot be achieved without this. Even if you're shy, remember that a simple smile can be a friendly, meaningful gesture. Don't isolate yourself by burying yourself in a work project. Don't avoid co-workers for long periods.

- ### *Step 3. Help others succeed.*

Let the adage "what goes around comes around" remind you that helping others to be successful is a way to ensure your own success. Volunteer to be a mentor for someone with promise or to train new workers in your department.

- ### *Step 4. Always listen to all sides.*

To be fair, you must listen to all sides of a discussion, a debate or an argument. You must be willing to weigh and balance all aspects of a situation. Listen more and talk less when others come to you. Don't try to change them. Instead, enjoy their opinions. You need to develop these crucial managerial and professional skills. They guarantee Equality and lay the foundation for effective communication.

- ### *Step 5. Know how to create a harmonious environment.*

The only prerequisites for creating a harmonious work environment are your belief in fairness and your willingness to act on that belief. This isn't always easy, but it can be achieved once you realize that only you can be responsible for your actions and only you can control your actions. You are responsible for the space or environment around you.

- ### *Step 6. Call it as you see it.*

When you accept that you are of equal value, you are not afraid to stand up for what you believe is true. In your workplace, it's important to state in a non-hostile way what you know to be true and to be willing to stick your neck out when necessary.

- ### *Step 7. Take a chance on others.*

To establish Equality, you must take a chance on others, giving them the opportunity to experience their own value. Be up front when you decide to take this type of

chance by informing the person of your confidence in her or
him and your willingness to support his or her effort to do
more.

- *Step 8. Take a chance on yourself.*

Think about the aspects of your workplace you wish
were different. Ask yourself the following questions:

1. How might I change this situation?
2. Am I willing to take action?
3. Will I retain my feeling of Equality if my
   suggestions or actions are not accepted or are
   unsuccessful?

If you can answer all three questions with a "yes," go
for it! Take that chance! Test your self-value. If you
answered "no" to one or more of the questions, go back to
all of the activities designed to create more internal balance
and determine which internal need is not being fulfilled.

- *Step 9. Redefine your definition of contribution.*

More than likely, your definition of contribution is too
narrow, limiting your experience of what you actually
contribute. If you underestimate the value of your contributions and put them down as unimportant or insubstantial,
you'll undermine your potential and value at work. Think of
a contribution as *anything* that you offer of yourself that is
either helpful, needed, wanted or simply given freely. This
will help you recognize how much you contribute on a
regular basis.

- *Step 10. Consider yourself first.*

Does this step sound contradictory to what you
believe being fair and equal is all about? As with Self-Love,
I reiterate, you can't give what you don't possess. So first
treat yourself as an individual of great value who's entitled
to Equality for no other reason than that you're worthy of it.

~ ~

Enjoy this wonderful feeling and all the good experiences derived from acting according to this belief. Enjoy the positive attitude that this feeling allows you to take to your workplace.

Notice how your positive attitude affects everyone around you.

How to Satisfy Your Need for Manipulation in Your Personal Life:

- *Step 1. Know what you want.*

It's important to know what you want before you set out to acquire it. Most people aren't sure exactly what they are seeking. It's impossible to know how to manipulate things in your favor if what you want is obscure or unidentified. Once you know what you want, be assertive. Don't hesitate to make your wants known, but do so in a courteous, cordial manner.

- *Step 2. Be specific.*

Don't cheat yourself out of details. Be specific with yourself while considering all of the facts, ramifications and outcomes. Know all that you can. Know before acting. Plan, organize and direct your thinking.

- *Step 3. Be confident within yourself.*

It's important to know how to Manipulate yourself in positive ways to ensure success in your life. To do this, you must learn to act in confident ways. Here are some tips to help you become more confident within:

  - Make sure your posture is good.
  - Make sure you breathe deeply using a regular rhythm.
  - Always hold your head high.
  - Never put yourself down, even in jest.

~ ~

- Take safe chances — chances that can't physically or emotionally harm you.
- If you feel you have a deficit, work to change
   it.
- Think of yourself as a lovable, happy,
   contented person. Then look in the mirror and
   see what that type of person looks like. Do
   you match the description? If you don't, try to
   figure out what expressions you need to
   change to accomplish that confident look.
   Fake it if you have to. Anything new is
   unnatural at first, but practice makes perfect!
- Learn information that makes you feel
   competent.
- Teach yourself a new word and its meaning
   once a week and stay updated with what's
   happening in the world.
- Think of yourself as a confident, well-
   rounded person. As you think, so shall it be.

- ***Step 4. Be honest with yourself.***

To meet your need for Manipulation without
Manipulating in a negative way, it's essential to understand
the motives or intentions behind your behavior. This takes
self-honesty. Question your intentions and motives before
taking any type of action. Acknowledge the fact that your
actions affect other people and anticipate what that effect
will be.

- ***Step 5. Be true to yourself.***

You need to understand your personal truth and live
that truth. If your personal truth is no longer a truth that you
are proud of or that you can appreciate, make sure you begin
the Manipulation process to change it. Holding on to out
dated values is a sign of rigidity that will manipulate you

rather than your environment. True freedom requires the flexibility to live your "new truth."

- **Step 6. Make your environment pleasant.**

Manipulate your environment so that it's pleasing and stimulating. For example, you can do something as simple as rearranging furniture, buying a picture that pleases you, or painting your favorite room a more relaxing color. It's important to create a sense of well-being and comfort around yourself. If your environment is chaotic, you can bet that your lifestyle will take on that chaos, as well.

- **Step 7. Learn the power of positive thinking.**

Treat yourself to a thought process that is uplifting, practical and rewarding. Manipulating your thoughts in a way to help you focus on the positive aspects of life is superior to dwelling on the negative. Here are five simple ways to help you make that shift in thought.

– When a negative thought creeps into your consciousness, say "STOP!" Then intentionally replace the negative thought with a positive thought.

– Each day, find a new way to change an ineffective behavior. Pick anything — this simple activity can be both challenging and fun.

– Focus on some recent situation or circumstance in your life which you perceive as negative. Try to find one aspect within this situation or circumstance that is positive. (Keep trying, it's in you).

– The next time you are with someone who is acting or talking in a negative way, concentrate in your own head on a positive trait about this person. While concentrating on this positive trait, think how loving he or she is.

~ ~

Do this even if you don't feel this way. See for yourself what happens.

   – Every day, find something positive about another person and bring it to his or her attention.

- ***Step 8. Get in touch with your own stimulus value.***

To empower yourself so your impact is positive, you must accept yourself as a person capable of Self-Power. You cannot Manipulate in an effective way if you are uncomfortable with Self-Power.

So accept your worth and enjoy the powerful experience of it.

- ***Step 9. Learn to depend on yourself.***

It feels good to be in charge of yourself and to know that you can create any reality that suits you. If you have never experienced your "in-chargeness," start now by balancing your checkbook, setting and accomplishing a goal or making a decision you've been avoiding. To succeed, remember the cliche: You have to crawl before you can walk.

- ***Step 10. Enjoy your independence.***

People who successfully Manipulate their lives in ways that are positive and effective strive for independence. They understand that being independent does not mean being isolated or distant from others. They acknowledge that true independence includes letting others into their lives without fearing loss of self.

They know that with independence comes self-control, self-appreciation, Self-Power, self-satisfaction and self-actualization.

How to Satisfy Your Need for Manipulation in Your Work Life:

- *Step 1. Choose your work.*

Most people spend the greater part of their waking hours at work. If only for this reason, choose a profession or job that you look forward to doing and that makes you feel good. If you are unhappy with your present work situation, ask yourself the following questions:

1. Would I like to change my career or place of employment?
2. Am I willing to do the research required to determine what it would take to make a change?
3. Do I feel I am willing to take a risk to make a change?
4. Do I have enough self-confidence to go for what I want?
5. Am I willing to invest whatever time is necessary (such as further education) to make this change?
6. Can I make this change without anyone else's support (financial or emotional)?
7. Am I willing to temporarily feel some discomfort and experience a possible loss of security in order to obtain something new?

You should be able to answer these basic questions with a firm "yes" before making any change. If you cannot answer "yes" to all of these questions, your need for Manipulation is low and needs more fulfillment and balance, or you really don't want to make a change.

- *Step 2. Practice your intuitiveness and use it.*

When you are interacting with others, pay close attention to your intuitive feelings or thoughts about them.

~ ~

One positive Manipulation skill is the ability to trust your gut feelings. This is a valuable asset. Test your intuitiveness by taking the risk to act on it. For starters, test it out in less consequential ways. Once you become trusting of your inner knowing, you will begin to use it to Manipulate whatever is necessary to ensure your success.

- *Step 3. Increase your personal visibility at work.*

To help achieve this, try to become part of the main traffic flow. It may be quieter away from the tumult of co-workers, but always choosing quiet makes you too invisible to exercise influence and have an impact on others. High visibility also involves more than physical space and sight.

Others may need to be reminded that you're important to them, so make yourself more critical to everyone by getting in the middle of the work flow, being sure to have information filtered through you rather than around you.

- *Step 4. Increase the visibility of your job.*

Expand the number of contacts you have within your organization. When you come up with a new idea, put it in writing and volunteer to make an oral presentation to others in the organization. When you accomplish something of value to the company, send out notices to your boss of that accomplishment or send a note to the person in charge of the company newsletter. Bosses often like this because it makes them and their department look better. Seek additional opportunities to increase personal name recognition at work.

- *Step 5. Enhance your persona in the organization.*

Develop an area in which you're the acknowledged expert. Expertise is a wonderful source of power and gives you an opportunity to Manipulate your environment in a way to help yourself and others. Any critical skill you can learn adds to your ability to make change. Another useful tool is to build up personal credits by extending more effort than expected when people ask you for help.

- *Step 6. Be aware of how you Manipulate.*

If you are unaware of how you Manipulate, you run the risk of manipulating in an unproductive or destructive way. To help you become more aware of your style of Manipulation, complete the following sentences:

1. I know my ability to influence others is good because when I influence them they ....
2. I know I am manipulating when I....
3. I feel comfortable manipulating when....
4. I believe it's okay to manipulate when....
5. I manipulate in the following ways (list three)....

- *Step 7. Increase your personal discretion and flexibility.*

Get rid of the routine activities. That will give you the time to expand what you do at work, giving you more variety and more influence. Get involved in new projects; participate in the early stages of the decision-making process when you have the opportunity to achieve the most impact over the project.

- *Step 8. Bring into your job a personal style that is difficult to replace.*

Avoid passive behavior that makes you inconspicuous. Be a team player. Make sure that your job functions are essential to the company. This places you in a stronger power position. In today's world of downsizing, this could be vital.

Some ways to accomplish this include obtaining advanced training, becoming more involved in professional organizations and exercising your own judgment.

~ ~

- ***Step 9. Build support groups.***

Creating a network of effective business friends who share common values not only protects you from damaging organizational politics, it also helps add to your own ability to effect practical change at work. When you want to implement a particular strategy, members of your network are a safe haven for testing your ideas. They also can offer support when you face heavy opposition. Meeting with your support group from time to time increases awareness of your proposed changes and helps reduce resistance to these ideas.

- ***Step 10. Manipulate to improve your life.***

Only exercise your Manipulation skills when there is an area of your life that needs improvement. Call on these wonderful skills to create healthy change, to enhance your environment, to bring out the best in others and to improve your work life in general. The skill of positive Manipulation makes the "good" difference.

Chapter Fourteen

Epilogue: A Final Thought

~ ~

I realize that we've reached the end of our journey together, but don't let that fact delude you into thinking that that's all there is. *Getting To Know You* is only the beginning of what can become a more satisfying and contented way of being. Applying what you learned from the GEM model, the self-reflective activities, the case examples, interviews and general information presented in this book is the key to stepping up to the next level of awareness and sensitivity. Some people refer to this next level as a more meditative state, a higher consciousness. It's also been identified as one's more spiritual self. But more important than identifying this higher level of self-growth is permitting yourself to experience this elevated level of learning, understanding, caring, loving, giving and receiving, which is best achieved by being non-judgmental and loving in your approach to yourself and others.

One of the major purposes of this book was to surface critical information and insight in order that you might gain

~ ~

a new perspective, a new way to think about yourself and others. Whatever lessons obtained from this material that help move you beyond your past will help you develop greater self-confidence and success.

If somehow you sense you are on a path different from where you've been before, a path that appears to be more spiritual and of a greater consciousness, allow yourself to become enlightened by this new experience and the positive thoughts, feelings and behavior that it produces. Overtly and covertly you'll find that this is the path that will help you communicate more peacefulness, tranquility, love and respect. You will treat yourself with greater kindness and thoughtfulness which is visible and can be felt by other people.

Self-growth journeys are never ending and time doesn't run out for insightful individuals who choose this personal path. These folks understand that time is never the "real" issue. They find the moments, the hours or even the days to commune with themselves in ways that allow them to experience the insights and the inner voice. As they grow and become more and more aware of the value of living their life from this more peaceful place within, they reap the abundant rewards generated by heightened creativity and serenity.

I hope the time you spent with this book and the information it offered you has helped to guide you to the realization that your potential is limitless. I hope you will continue creating self-reflective and meditative practices that manifest for you more and more knowledge, knowledge that allows you to keenly observe and be sensitive to all things of importance in your life. Let your willingness to search, to learn and to experience be your evidence that within your person your nature is one that thirsts for better ways to grow and spiritually unfold.

It's exciting once you accept that you have the power to create personal change in your life. Even more exciting is learning the value and benefits of dealing with others and life situations by first confronting past history, which includes old messages, old beliefs, biases and prejudices, and old behavior.

I want you to know that spending time with you, and guiding you through GEM was a gift to me. Sharing information in new and different ways is always adventurous. If you only gained one insight from this book, my wish would be that that one insight is to never stop learning and stretching yourself.

And just as your taking this journey was a present to me, the GEM model's present to you is the reminder to self-reflect, reevaluate, redefine and redirect. You have a personal responsibility to set straight what isn't right and to create positive options, choices and solutions. Remind yourself that when you eliminate bias and prejudicial thinking, you free yourself from any negative beliefs and values that interfere with your spiritual development and your overall effectiveness.

The time is right for you to let your spiritual self guide you to greater achievements and more understanding. Use all that you have learned. Develop yourself and believe in your ability to tap into a broader perspective of your world and the people in it. This is what it will take if you want to become more effective. Try to stay centered and focus on the following:

Have undying faith in yourself, even when your world appears to be offering you little hope.

Turn inward and attend to your internal needs.

Create internal balance.

~ ~

Put whatever new ideas you have learned into action.

Go forward, looking back only as a way to gain information or to heal old pain that is standing in your way.

Accept the fact that you are a loving, creative, intelligent person who has the capability to enjoy life and receive abundant rewards.

Become powerful through self-knowledge, self-awareness, sensitivity and self-respect.

Remember, in order to do this you must know how to satisfy your need for Self-Love, Self-Power, Intimacy, Solitude, Equality and Manipulation, and you must know how to create internal balance between them.

Good luck in your new endeavors. I encourage you to let your own motivation take over by exploring and satisfying your curiosity about yourself. Don't be afraid to unlock the door to your feelings. It's very powerful when you can express exactly what it is you feel. Why shouldn't you have this freedom of expression?

It's time for us to part, I trust you will choose your own unique way from here, never forgetting that who you are is who you choose to be.

Don't be afraid to experience a new you! You are a real GEM!

To arrange for speeches, workshops or special presentations, Kay Francis may be reached at:

Kay Francis
2699 Stirling Road, Suite A105
Fort Lauderdale, Florida 33312

Fax – 305-926-0272
Phone – 305-922-7625

To order additional copies of

Getting To Know You

Please send _____ copies at $14.95 for each book, plus $3.50 shipping and handling for each book.

Enclosed is my check or money order of $_____
or [ ] Visa [ ] MasterCard
#_____ Exp. Date ____/____
Signature _____

Name _____
Street Address _____
City _____
State _____ Zip _____
Phone _____

(Advise if recipient and shipping address are different from above.)

For credit card orders call:
1-800-895-7323

or
Return this order form to:

BookPartners
P.O. Box 922
Wilsonville, OR 97070